# NEW LEASE
## ON
## LIFE

*The Story of a City Family Who Quit the Rat Race*

**RANDOM HOUSE   NEW YORK**

# NEW LEASE
## ON
## LIFE

*nd Moved to a Ranch in Wyoming*

# OTIS CARNEY

*To Teddy*

to be nobody-but-yourself—
in a world which is doing its best,
night and day,
to make you everybody else—
means to fight the hardest battle
which any human being can fight;
and never stop fighting.

—E.E. Cummings

# FOREWORD

"Some circumstantial evidence is very strong," Thoreau said, "as when you find a trout in the milk."

Now, this is not a fish story, but when you up and leave the city in the middle of your life, quit the Big Game and move to a ranch in Wyoming, you've got some explaining to do. Your friends think you've escaped, retired or gone mad. Anyway, you're out of it. You've taken the easy way out.

In certain respects, I suppose we have. Our routine is pretty much a succession of days where nothing changes except the seasons, where the news of the world rarely leaks in; and by then we've lost the continuity of it and don't care.

But escape is a joyous word. It means going free. And here's where the real fight begins.

When you're in your mid-forties, you don't just cut yourself in two, pack your bags and get out. It's a matter of values, distance, a tearing that takes years and is never quite done. You have to rip up roots that were bred into you and put on the new man. And even if you put on nice soft old Levis instead of Brooks Brothers flannels, that new suit is going to chafe and sometimes downright hurt.

It's a pretty strange culture mix, me, at forty-nine, chasing cows around the sagebrush. I'm at best a suburban who used to think grass was something to lose golf balls in. I couldn't rope a steer if he lay down and stuck his feet in the air. Even the trout: I love to catch them out of the beautiful river in my front yard, but I can't stand the taste of the damn things. I wish they had a zippered skin so I could fill them with tunafish. In light of such incongruity, the logical question is: What the hell brought me here?

I wish I had an easy answer. Or that I could point to one emotion-packed moment when I knew I was fed up with the rat race and said, Goodbye! I'm getting out! But it didn't happen like that. There's a sneaky little rationale you build and hide behind, at least I did. You have a pleasant life where you are, you let obligations crust over you until they're a dead weight. You've been educated and trained onto the twentieth-century economic treadmill. You know you can't possibly get off. As Ralph Waldo Emerson said, "God gives to every man a choice. He can have truth, or he can have repose. He cannot have both."

And truth must be the stimulus of the city, kids in what's called the right schools, being on top of things, glittering like a sports car on the freeway, hurrying to where the action is.

For many people, the rationale works, brings happiness and productive lives. Oh sure, at times everybody wonders whether the other fellow's grass isn't greener. Your particular rut suddenly seems overwhelming, your life a nonsense of trivia. You want to bug out, grab a slow boat to Tahiti. But then maturity takes over, caution bred in wisdom. The yearning passes and you just take a train home.

You're lucky if you can get away with it. I tried for a long time. But there was a collision point ahead for me, and maybe Mark Twain put his finger on it when he said: "You are the maker of the dream."

That was my siren song. The dream I wanted didn't fit the world I'd been raised in. So I kept ducking it and equivocating until finally I had to make a choice.

This book is that story.

Otis Carney

Cora, Wyoming
September, 1970

# NEW
## LEASE ON LIFE

Including wilderness that has
not yet been surveyed, Sublette
County, Wyoming, has a land area of
approximately 5000 square miles. That
makes it slightly larger than the state of
Connecticut. In the entire county, there are
68,976 cattle, 3038 horses and 3778 people.

Actually, the cattle and horse figures are probably low. They come from the tax rolls, and everybody
has a few calves and colts around that don't seem worth
mentioning. The people count is also a little uncertain.
Some suspect it's dropped from the last census.

In Sublette County there's a place called Cora. It consists of
a log general store with a post office inside, has a zip code and a
resident population of three. We get our mail here, but we live,
like most ranchers, far off in the sagebrush, beyond where the
pavement ends. Our particular ranch lies in a valley that has no
name. People call it "up country" or "the far side of Black Butte."
You can't get here by commercial airline. We're not on an air-
way; few jets rumble overhead. We're also the farthest settlement in the United States from a railroad. The Union Pacific
tracks are a hundred and twenty miles south; Salt Lake City, two
hundred and fifty.

But from where you live to here isn't really a matter of miles.
It's time. You have to go back to the nineteenth century, forget
your huff and haste. Maybe that's why so few come. It's a long
trip back, learning to live an old way.

Each year in the spring our world opens up; life begins.
We've been feeding cattle with teams and sleighs since early
November. But now it's May 1, only a foot and a half of snow left,
water trickling out and greening the grass in a few bare spots. We
still have to use skis to get from our house across the bridge to
our truck. Then, in four-wheel drive and chains, we splatter and
skid up a mudbog road twenty-eight miles to town. We buy a
thousand yearling cattle, borrow a small fortune on them, and
pray.

We wonder, on days like this, about the gamble we've made,
coming here.

But not for long.

When I walk outside tonight, the world seems serenely simple in the quiet Wyoming dusk.

The Green River, a few yards below me, lies still-silver, smoking in the cold. It's nine above zero, ice crusting the riverbanks, but even now the brook and rainbow trout are starting to move. They make soft rings on the water as they dapple up to feed. A beaver drags willow branches across to the far shore. In this same place his ancestors have been building the same house for uncounted centuries. Men came here in 1805 to trap, club, shoot the beaver, plunder him for the fur hats of Europe. After years of ravaging the river, these men walked the mountains and deserts all the way to the Pacific Coast, guided the wagon trains and opened the manifest destiny of a nation. The beaver outlived them all.

In the last light I hear the crack of a gun. Davy, my foreman's boy, is running down from the ranch bridge to fish out a muskrat he's shot. He'll get fifty cents for the skin and use the money for the next installment in his taxidermy course. The gunshot has awakened the twilight. There's a sudden warbling, so powerful that it echoes far off in the dark lodgepole pines of the mountains. Out in the hay meadows two stalky gray shapes are running; then they lift, the dying rays tinting their wings vermilion. They're immense, ungainly, like deer in flight. But they soar now: sandhill cranes. The pioneers slaughtered them for their meat, the Mexicans scatter-gunned them until they were almost gone. Thirty years ago, strangely, they showed up here, a few at a time, until they began to come in flocks and lay their eggs as big as softballs on our hay meadows. Farther, out of distant loops in the river, geese have risen, honking, and are silhouetted against the aspen hills. Mallards, widgeon, teal dart across the paling sky, set their wings and home down for the night. Out in the sagebrush that's just now protruding from snow, three moose hurry off on the trot. Hardly breaking their stride, they step across a barbed-wire fence and pause, looking back toward the rifle sound. They're not afraid of it, just curious and lordly as only a moose can be. They'll take a last look around before they plunge into the willow bottoms and begin to calve.

The light has gone now. I can barely see a smudge moving to the top of a ridge. The smudge howls, and I smile. They've tried to wipe him out too, using sophisticated poisons and gunning him from airplanes. But the coyote still lives on our land, and in the quiet night, has the last laugh at all of us.

To watch Nature struggle in birth, death and certain rebirth, this is the spring here, and in it I see again how small I am, how little my strivings really matter.

This, too, is the peace, so far off once, so long to find.

I didn't have any idea such a world existed. Yet I was close to it on an afternoon in October, 1955. We were rumbling across Wyoming on the Union Pacific. "Westward, I go free," Thoreau said, and we thought we were. We'd made a big decision. We were moving from Chicago to Los Angeles, going by train because we had all the luggage of uprooting a household. Besides, I love trains, the lonely bleat of the diesel horn and the land unfolding slow enough so you can see its history.

I'd taken Teddy, my wife, and our three sons, Tom, John and Peter, up into the Vistadome. The kids had never been West before. They were civilized little suburbanites, pink faces, their hair in Cromwell-style bangs. They wore Oxford-gray short-pants suits and round white collars. They'd look out at the empty desert and say, "Tell us what happened here, Dad!"

I was as lost as they were, but I did have the Union Pacific route guide. It mentioned the Oregon Trail, running somewhere in the smoky foothills to the north. So I'd start spinning wagon-train yarns until a little hand would flash up: "Hey! There's a cowboy!"

"A really cowboy," Pete announced gravely.

As the sky darkened, Teddy and I ordered a cocktail. Beyond Evanston, Wyoming, the Wasatch range pinched in. The tracks ran along the Bear River and I noticed a man in waders, fishing for trout. By now the kids were fidgeting; the scenery was gone, they wanted to eat. Maybe it was the closeness I felt or bourbon emotion, but I said, "You know, boys, after we're settled in California, we might get a little place where we could have horses and dogs . . ."

"A ranch?" John asked. "Like on TV?"

"Oh no, nothing that big. Just a way to get out into these mountains and streams. We ought to do that. There's a lot of things we can do that we didn't, back home."

Their eyes gleamed against the glass of the Vistadome. They

5

didn't know what I meant, and neither did I, but it sounded like some kind of liberation. And we needed one right then, to keep us from looking back at what we'd left behind.

Johnny called them "The Big Family": my parents, brothers, sister and their children. We'd said goodbye to them the night before in Lake Forest, a suburb of Chicago. I'd grown up here, worked here, and the kids had started their first schools. When we got ready to leave, everybody gathered around the car. Teddy cried, then Mother. My father walked slowly away. A few friends predicted that we'd be back in a year or so, but all of us at the car knew we wouldn't. This time it was for keeps.

Teddy finished her drink, said she'd take the kids into the diner. I ordered a second bourbon and soon I was alone in the Vistadome; dark outside, distant lights rising and fading. And I saw clearly then the force that had put me on that train. It frightened me too, because it was rushing me toward strange places, and wouldn't again let me find peace in the old, established way.

As far back as I could remember, I'd had two goals: I wanted to be a writer and live on the land, far from the crowd. Now, that's a nice romantic notion, but it didn't really connect to anything I'd ever known. In the suburb where I grew up, life was eminently pleasant. We had a close, happy family, security, friends. The orientation of my boyhood was definitely toward business; people rode trains into Chicago, worked hard. I respected them.

But then, when I was sixteen, we bought a little farm out in the Illinois cornfields west of town. I began spending a lot of time there with horses and bird dogs. I also took a fling at writing and did a "novel" on the Civil War. It was lumpy and god-awful, yet the thrill of putting down words hooked me. I even fell in love with the heroine, a brown-haired southern belle whose family had a plantation. I resolved someday to marry her.

Perhaps in normal times I would have grown up out of the writing phase and got conformity. But this was 1939. On the weekend I arrived at Princeton, war was declared in Europe. We knew right then we were racing the clock and we began jamming in all the living we could. We played games, chased girls and made some lifelong friends. Along the way I did try to get in the Creative Writing seminar but my grades weren't good enough. Then I began doing stories for the humor magazine, the

*Tiger.* On a Friday, I was elected chairman of it. We had a party over the weekend and woke up Sunday to Pearl Harbor.

Actually, many of us had looked forward to the prospect of war. We saw it with all the glamour of a Lafayette Escadrille movie. And we felt we needed an escape like this, because we knew we were being trained into the same social-economic pecking order as the Princeton classes before us. The "country house society," Scott Fitzgerald called it. So give us a fling overseas, and when the fighting was done we'd come home to the law firms, banks and brokerage houses.

Well, the war we got had a new script, and many of us wouldn't be the same after it. Within a month I'd quit Princeton and joined naval aviation. During flight training a boyhood friend, Chuck Spalding, and I decided, pretty much for the hell of it, that we'd write a novel about our experiences. Chuck was a born humorist and the majority of the book was his. But the real miracle was that it found a publisher and a ready-made audience. It seemed as if everybody had a relative learning to fly, and after you've knitted a scarf and a wool hat, what do you send him except a book that might make him laugh? So *Love at First Flight* took off, became a best seller, and for me, a kind of albatross.

Because it was too much, too soon, success in writing on a silver platter, and I kept wanting to build on the bonanza. During the two years I was flying around the Pacific in the Marine Corps, I hammered out newspaper articles that got published, short stories that didn't, and finally started a novel that grew to a couple of hundred pages of original manuscript. I was typing it under our plane on Peleliu Island when a Japanese ammunition dump exploded fifty yards away. We were so frantic to get the plane out of there that we roared up the engines, jumped the chocks and blew my brainchild all over the island, never to return.

About that time I was struck by a quick, terrifying insight. One afternoon in 1945, I was standing in an outdoor shower on Guam, watching silver B-29's lumbering overhead for a fire-bomb raid on Japan. Suddenly I heard an anguished roar, looked up. One of the planes had dropped out of formation and was rushing directly toward me, writhing, losing altitude. Two engines on the left wing were trailing smoke, the stricken sheaf of metal flashing not twenty feet over my head. The pilot and the eleven men in the plane were trying desperately to reach the airfield behind me.

I snatched my towel and ran toward them, didn't get fifty yards from the shower before the B-29 crashed in a sickening thunder and erupted in flame.

I ran as close as I could. Machine-gun ammunition, fire bombs were exploding, the heat belching out, searing my face. I could do nothing but watch the men in flight suits, clawing the plexiglass blisters, burning alive.

I carried them with me for a long time. There, but for the grace of God, went I. And then the memory hardened until it was a pledge: I had one life. If I got back to live it, the hell with what the world said. I'd use it my way, my dream.

Now, as I rumbled along on the Union Pacific, that vision seemed very distant. As with most insights, so much had happened to block it out: circumstances beyond our control.

The war ended and we all began to run very fast: make up for the lost years, get a degree, a job. I went back to finish at Princeton, still hoping to be a writer and not having a notion how to do it. On a night in June, 1946, I decided to crash a debut party in New Jersey. I really didn't want to go but my roommate talked me into it. After trying to get a highball at the bar . . . they only served champagne . . . I drifted out on the dance floor and cut in on a girl I'd never seen before.

We danced for a while, and finally I directed her to the ladies' room, which was on the second floor of the old Colonial house. As I waited for her at the bottom of the stairs, some of my college friends came up and wanted to know if I'd lucked into anything. Well, I was a little sheepish. This girl was three days out of Foxcroft, certainly no more than eighteen. A cradle robber, my friends called me. But I said no, and, using the quaint vernacular of the day, added, "She's got a lot of shots. Look."

I pointed up, and there my discovery stood, all grace and poise at the top of the stairs. "Not bad," the boys murmured.

She took the first dainty step down, tripped, and rolled the entire staircase in an arm-flailing ball of white tulle.

Well, I got the poor flustered thing picked up and brushed off. The boys smirked away. An exact year from that night I was brushing rice off her, and in all the years since, she hasn't made a false step. That was Teddy, the luckiest trip of my life.

Who saw her in the dream? I surely didn't. Marriage was the

last thing in the world I'd thought about or needed right then. And the spooky part of it was that Teddy seemed to have stepped right out of the pages of my Civil War novel. She was brown-haired, from an old family in Memphis, Tennessee. They even had a plantation, sold it a week before the wedding, now that the Yankee carpetbaggers had come down.

But the real blessing of Teddy was something I didn't expect. She had a natural spirituality, and never cared about being like everybody else, doing what the group did. It was her courage and sense of freedom that helped, slowly, to change our lives.

From the beginning, she wanted me to write, and was willing to do anything to help me. I'd started out as a newspaper reporter in Minneapolis. We had Tom and John; we were surrounded by wonderful friends, all of us shelling out babies like popcorn. We were optimistic, young, everybody a success and in love. No more wars, nobody saving the world; we were making our own.

I kept writing, pecked out two novels, sometimes in the newsroom at the paper but mostly at night after work. When the rejection slips came, I'd just get mad and start another one. Then I jumped into television because it seemed to be the coming medium. I formed a producing company that later went broke, but it did move us back to Chicago. We rented a house in Lake Forest: familiar surroundings, family, friends. With my experience in TV, I went to work for an advertising agency, writing commercials. We had Peter and the Good Life.

My paycheck bought a lot of golf balls and snowsuits and put the kids into schools. The years began flicking away like little pieces of cardboard punched from my commuting ticket. And slowly I realized that my confrontation was here. I had to face it now.

I'd been trying to write books, and had failed at it for nearly ten years. But still I wanted to do it. I wanted the freedom of a writer's life.

I wasn't an organization man, never could be. I'd sit in my office in the lonely slump hours of the afternoon, look out at the gray Chicago River and at the murky office lights in the other skyscrapers. And I'd wonder how many of those people liked what they were doing. Would they quit if they could?

Then, one morning in the fall, I happened to take a couple of agency executives duck-hunting. Out in the yellow, frosty marsh we had a fine shoot, picked our ducks, drank a beer and never wanted to leave. But that afternoon important clients were coming to the office. We raced into Chicago, gulped down a martini lunch. After it we had a three-hour meeting, fifteen of us listening to a refrigerator commercial I'd written. What we were trying to decide was whether the sound of the defroster should be played as a *whooosh* or a *whaash.*

I never knew how it came out. Because that night, with Teddy's urging, I made up my mind to quit and be a free-lance writer. "Dammit," she said, "you have to."

I set up shop in our guest room, and in my new-found freedom I ambled down one day to a local stationery store. As I bought typewriter paper, a charming older woman came up to me. I'd known her all my life. In apparent concern she said, "Why, Otis, you're not sick, are you?"

"No."

"Then why aren't you in town, at work?"

The question seemed perfectly natural. Everybody commuted to the city. "Well," I said, "I work at home. I'm writing."

She looked at me blankly. She was earnestly trying to figure it out. But nobody you knew "wrote." It didn't exist in this world. "Well," she said and smiled. "I do hope you get better. This flu is a nasty bug."

I knew right then it wasn't going to be easy. Every morning when the commuting train left, its whistle sent a guilty chill down my spine. In the city, balance sheets were hammering through printing machines. What did mine say? That I was going to support myself in a fancy suburb by *writing?* How'd they take that one out on the first tee, after the first year and a few more unpublished epics? I was afraid to look. I kept staring at the typewriter, with Teddy encouraging me, until finally I began seeing a novel about people in a suburb. My friends, my background; I loved them, I'd played the game with them. Still, I knew that some of them, like me, were beginning to die slowly inside, leading lives of quiet desperation, asking, even then: Was the reward, getting to the top of the heap, going to be worth it?

Though I was convinced there had to be a book in the security quest of our postwar generation, I wasn't ready to write it. I groped, fumbled, and finally, when my confidence was gone, I started cranking out magazine articles, sales films and even TV commercials to help pay the bills. In short, I had my craft and my freedom, and I was floundering in it.

Then the phone rang.

No actor in a Greek tragedy ever needed a *deus ex machina* more. Mine happened to be Louis de Rochemont, a movie producer for whom I'd worked briefly while I courted Teddy. Louis was putting together a film in the new Cinerama process, and wanted me to join him.

We bundled up the kids and hurried to New York, moved into an apartment hotel. What followed was a year of challenge, thrill and insanity. I helped write *Cinerama Holiday,* then went out on location as the producer of the American sequences. This meant sixty employees, a caravan of trucks, advance men, publicity men, production managers. Wildly, we began leapfrogging the country: marching bands in New Orleans, herding cattle with Apaches in Arizona; we commandeered a county fair in New Hampshire and set a casino on fire in Las Vegas. The idea of Cinerama was to put the audience in the picture, and we rocked relentlessly down San Francisco hills in cable cars, rattled through the Rockies on a special train of the California Zephyr. For three weeks we took over an aircraft carrier in the Atlantic, filmed the thundering Blue Angels, shot down drone planes and moved destroyers around like boy admirals in a bathtub. For a finale, we filmed President Eisenhower, and Mrs. Eisenhower made a quick wardrobe change so we could take her picture in her new pink hat.

It was hard to come back down to earth after Cinerama; I found I loved the excitement of film. It certainly seemed a helluva lot pleasanter than a lonely life in a garret, writing a book. But the problem in working on big location pictures meant I had to spend a lot of time away from Teddy and the kids. Once, in fact, when I came home to Lake Forest, the boys were off down in the garden; I glanced at them and asked Teddy who the little friend with bangs was, playing with Tom and Pete.

John, she said.

If this was to be the price of film-making, I wasn't ready to pay it. Yet there did seem to be a compromise. Go to Hollywood. There, as far as I could tell, you could still write films and lead a relatively normal life. I began making trips to the Coast, wondering if I'd have the courage to yank us up again and move.

Then, unexpectedly, the choice confronted us.

In New York, during Cinerama, I'd gotten to know the president of the advertising agency for which I'd once worked. He was an outstanding man, a charmer and a visionary. He wanted to do a new kind of television program that would dramatize great American stories and film them in the places where they had happened. Because of my Cinerama experience, he took me on as a consultant to create the show. We worked together for some months, and when my outline was completed, we sat down in his office high above Lexington Avenue. "Look," he said, "the only way we're going to get this thing done is for you to come in here, in the company." He offered me a vice-presidency, salary, stock options, a generous future dumped in my lap. I'd get a house up in Connecticut for Teddy and the kids, do this show and others, and find the proper Hollywood studios to produce them.

It meant simply . . . and he said it: Give up the creative dream. Everybody had to make this decision sooner or later. He'd made it himself. Because the power and control, the moving of creative forces was up here in the executive suite. You had to be in the organization to do it.

Strangely, the choice was so clear-cut that Teddy and I didn't agonize over it long. We knew we'd had that life, in a smaller way, in Chicago. I'd broken with it once, came up empty, but still I felt I had to keep trying to write on my own. I told the agency president this. He was disappointed but nevertheless wanted to go ahead with the show. He agreed to move me to Hollywood, where I'd continue as a consultant. Teddy and I hurried out, rented a house in Beverly Hills, swimming pool and palm trees.

As I sat in the Vistadome that night, I felt confident that it had all worked out for the best now. I didn't seem to have the temperament or ability book-writing required. Television was a creative, economically fruitful compromise. It made sense for us; it was the challenge I needed.

The future resolved so rosily, I went down to dinner; Teddy and I took the kids back to the compartment and started putting them to bed. We were past Salt Lake now, but the boys were still peering out at a very dark West, wondering what lay ahead. Then the porter poked his face in. "Better give me a wake-up time for the morning. Next stop," he said and grinned, "Los Angeles!"

I earnestly hoped it would be my last.

We'd been warned that when you move to Beverly Hills, California, you go into cultural shock. It's like a bad case of the bends. You need a decompression chamber, and without it "the only way to survive," my friend from the East shrieked, "is to get a lovely house, pull it over your ears and hide."

"Then what?" I asked her.

"Wait awhile. I've been through a lot of cases like yours. It usually takes about a year, and suddenly you realize you've fallen in love with this corny, freaky, unbelievable life. There's no place in the world better to live! You watch now. See if you don't have exactly that reaction."

I was thinking about her the first Christmas Eve we spent in California. We went swimming in the late afternoon, heard the bees in the bougainvillaea. Then some friends invited us out for a "Christmas Show." The festivities were taking place in a View Tract called Panorama City. In an asphalt parking lot behind a supermarket, we found Santa all right, but the eighty-degree heat had shifted his cargo. He was huffing, sweating, and the silver spangles they'd sprayed on him for snow were running down his cheeks. Because of the crowd, our kids couldn't get close to him, so they wandered off through a forest of three-foot-high Christmas trees. These, too, had been sprayed, electric-blue, crimson, pale pink. At the far end of the wilderness was the big attraction all the kids were running toward: a mangy deer on a chain, sprayed silver and with papier-mâché horns.

I glowered at Teddy. "Is this supposed to be Christmas?"

"I know. We should have gone home, skated, played in the snow."

"Well, what the hell are we doing in this dump?"

She smiled. "Giving it a year, remember?"

It was one of my lowest times. I chafed, bucked and pined, and what made it worse, Teddy was already loving it. You could dump her in Siberia or the Sahara and the next morning she'd be hanging pictures or out planting flowers. "The trouble with you," she'd say, "is that you're spoiled and demanding."

"You're damn right I am. I hate living jammed up cheek to jowl with a lot of morons, loud cars and bratty kids."

Then I'd tick off my grievances: we were paying a fortune in rent, had a psychopath for a landlord. The house was in a steep canyon where the sun shone two hours a day and then the snails took over. The only place I could play ball with my boys was a tiny pad cut out of a hillside. A good solid bunt would leap the edge and down into the poison oak, and furthermore, the neighbor who owned the pad delighted in coming out in his undershirt and running us off.

"If we're patient enough," Teddy said, "we'll be able to buy a house someplace with privacy. I know we can."

"And how are we going to pay for it?"

"You'll figure something out," she'd say, and then go back to her nesting.

I suppose a writer's wife has to learn early to cope with moods like these. But the facts now really weren't very optimistic. When I'd left New York, the advertising agency, networks and sponsor had been busily negotiating the Americana TV show. Six months later they were still negotiating, trying to get action, a straight yes or no. But in show business, as in Eliot, things don't end with a bang, merely a whimper. The networks refused to put the program on the air because they didn't feel it was commercial enough. (What they really wanted was a share of ownership, but we didn't learn that until it was too late.) Anyway, the project bombed and I was a barnacle who went down with the dream boat. So there we were in Beverly Hills with no visible means of support. All right, I thought, I can still write for television. I offered my services.

Resounding silence.

I tried this agent, that agent, wrote outlines, treatments, I met people, circulated, leaned on my Cinerama experience, and didn't get in a single door. But then one opened that had been there all the time, and I hadn't seen it. That was the door of a tiny fiberglass hut at our swimming pool, where there was only room for the hot-water heater, my typewriter and me. In fact, it was like getting into the cockpit of a plane for a long and dreary trip. But I was desperate enough that I knew I had to write something, and the only thing around was the book I'd failed at back in Lake Forest. It told of the world I'd left behind—men in big corporations, commuting trains, golf games, the chase for security and, too often, the myth it turned out to be. I called it *When the Bough*

*Breaks,* which meant, in a way, the growing-up.

To my amazement, the book not only found a publisher but a book club as well, made the *New York Times* best-seller list for a heady few weeks, then went into reprints and sold quite a respectable number of copies.

By now we'd been in California eighteen months, but I wasn't counting the time any more. Because, as our eastern friend had predicted, we'd fallen in love with the place. On an afternoon in April we drove up Benedict Canyon into the wrinkled soft Santa Monica mountains. Our real estate agent had heard of a house that had to be sold quickly to liquidate an estate. As we came up the driveway, a covey of quail skittered across; then we lifted onto a beautiful isolated hilltop where you couldn't hear the cars or smell the smog. I never looked at a closet or bathroom, just told Teddy this was it. We bought it that afternoon and pulled it over our ears.

We were home to stay.

We had seven acres, a pool, all the beauty and privacy you'd want, less than fifteen minutes from Beverly Hills. We put in a tennis court; Teddy gardened until she was sunburned and exhausted; we planted Monterrey pines, bougainvillaea, roses. It was going to be our paradise and refuge too, and we couldn't believe our luck at finding it.

What we'd stumbled onto was known in local parlance as a "Movie Star View Estate." You referred to it as the Hedy Lamar–Humphrey Bogart–Lauren Bacall–Robert Newton place. Apparently Miss Lamar, fresh from her nude dip in *Ecstasy,* had pioneered up Benedict Canyon when it was still a dirt road. In 1941 MGM homesteaded her on top of our ridge—wild land, ultra-private—and she built there, of all things, a pristine white New England cottage. She was unmarried then; whether she swam skinny in our pool I never knew, but it was fun to think about. In fact, it was hard to imagine her as the type who would grub around chicken houses and stables. Yet she must have had the land in her because she built some farm buildings before she left. Then the Bogart–Bacall regime carried on as the next country squires. In the evenings Bogart would curl up with a toddy and a rifle and pop off targets of opportunity, mainly deer. We found their legs and skulls in the basement. When the Bogarts finally moved to a more civilized address in Holmby Hills, Robert Newton, the distinguished British actor, took over. He could never spend enough time there, we heard, but, like the other tenants, he cherished the moments he did have. One morning, while we were living in our scruffy rented house, we heard an ambulance siren wailing up the canyon. Newton had had an asthma attack and died in his bedroom. We bought from his widow.

In our first flush of love for the place, I did overlook a few details that apparently terrified sensible California house-hunters. Coming from the Illinois prairies, I'd never paid much attention to brush fires. Kid stuff, stamp 'em out with your shoes. Well, here, our home and castle was what the local fire department called a "bird's nest." Perched atop a ridge, surrounded by explosive native mesquite, it was the textbook example of where not to live in fire season. We began majoring in Instant Terrifying Evacuation. First, one New Year's Eve, Benedict Canyon exploded in flames. A policeman tried to keep us from going home, but with the kids there, I ran the roadblock. Next year Bel Air torched up to the west of us. We watched it on TV while we packed our worldly goods. As the mushroom cloud of smoke darkened the sky, an impressionable young man parked within sight of our house and started his own fire. I raced around setting my hoses, but you couldn't have dampened a washrag with the pressure they had. The fire-bombing planes zoomed in and doused that one and the cops put the crackpot away.

By necessity, some of our best friends became insurance men; they had to go as far as Lloyd's of London to get us even minimum coverage. Our existence, in fact, was almost Biblical: fire, flood and pestilence. We discovered that Miss Lamar had built her graceful three-quarters-of-a-mile driveway directly over the area's largest watershed. In bad storms, subterranean springs filled up and erupted like Old Faithful right through our pavement. After we'd lost a massive roadgrader in a bog by the mailbox, we repaved with what I'm sure was platinum. And in the torrential rains the next winter an ivy-covered bank loosened and dumped thirty tons of earth on the tennis court. We began to wonder whether we shouldn't own our own bulldozer, rather than buying somebody else's on time.

Then in the spring the beautiful hills would bloom with mustard, lush vines of poison oak . . . and rattlesnakes. All of us learned to bag rattlers with the weapon at hand, usually a tennis racquet. Teddy opened a downstairs closet once and got hers with a shoetree. We'd heard that the Newtons entertained one snake in the living room; they called the cops and a quick-draw officer plugged it, leaving a .38 hole in the floor.

Next came the infestation of civet cats. This is a California euphemism for just plain skunk. I know because I tried to catch one with a fishing net and a crowbar in our silver closet. I'd heard if you could hold their tail down, they wouldn't spray. Don't believe it. For several weeks I'd sit at the breakfast table with a BB gun; we'd open the kitchen drawers and our skunk family would pop up like toast. I'd ping away, usually missing. Then I tried to get the exterminators to take over, but there's an odd California law that protects civet cats. By now it was them or us, so on the sneak I hired a boozy old illegal trapper. He put some foul baits in the basement, grunted incantations, and our visitors disappeared. But the coyotes stayed on. We were surrounded in the hills by jabbering packs that would howl you out of a sound sleep. One bunch had gobbled up Newton's dog. They also liquidated the cats we bought to keep the snake population under control. They or something did; you never knew just what to expect in the jungles of Benedict Canyon.

One night, in fact, our baby-sitter and her boyfriend were watching TV. They began hearing a noise that didn't fit the show, and finally went to the front door. Six feet away a mountain lion was clawing at our rubber tree. I give Hedy Lamar due credit for her courage in homesteading, but she hadn't tamed all the land. We were carrying on.

We had a helluva good time at it. The house was a superb place to raise kids: no traffic, neighbor-proof and serene. We did have to import friends for the kids, but the trip seemed worth it. They'd camp with our boys in the hills, play ball on the tennis court and have riotous splashing pool parties. Our kids were perpetually sunburned and healthy, no more snowsuits to mess with. They were trooping happily and we thought productively through the parochial school in Beverly Hills. I'd take them to the ocean or out into the neighboring mountains to hunt quail. We had bird dogs and a monkey, our own citrus trees and flowers enough to fill the house. I suppose we could even have kept horses. A few families nearby had them. But Hedy Lamar's stables had fallen down by now; I'd bulldozed them away. For all the beauty of the canyon, I could feel the city closing in. The idea of clopping around on pavement wasn't the kind of ride I wanted.

Teddy and I made dozens of friends from many different groups. What struck us most about Los Angeles was the stimulation and excitement of life there. Some of our friends were in show business but many more worked in other fields. You had little of the stultification of a suburb where you usually saw the same faces every Saturday night. Because we "passed" in so many circles, we were continually being exposed to new ideas and experiences, some of them nutty but all rewarding in a way. By Teddy's standards we went out too much. She's a conscientious hostess, loves to cook and give dinner parties, so we paid everybody back in a social life we soon realized could eat you alive. But the parties we did have were fun.

Teddy also loves music and became a regular at the symphony and the opera. We played a lot of tennis together, took long walks down through the quiet hills. I joined a duck club, and often Teddy and I made other trips to hunt down in Mexico. It seemed in fact that there were more diversions than we had time for: out-of-town guests, big bashy parties and little ones, visits to people's ranches or their yachts. Yet some of the best times we had were *en famille.* Because there wasn't a country club structure for us and most of our friends, we often got together with everybody's kids. Curious, that in racy big-city Los Angeles, you seemed to spend more time with your children than most people do in suburbs across the land.

Yet for all the apparent glamour and excitement of our life, we were an archaic bunch by some standards. Teddy and I weren't quite old enough to be Lawrence Welk people but our values seemed like it. We were still married and very much in love. We had two vehicles, a perpetually three-year-old Ford or Chevy station wagon and one escape car which got me out in the mountains hunting and fishing. The first of these was a blue International Travelall, a clanking monster that had four-wheel drive and a permanent layer of adobe dust. Tom, learning to drive, had kicked the door in to punish the truck for stalling on him. A few nights later I drove it to a fancy movie party in Bel Air, arriving behind a Cadillac and ahead of a Dual Ghia. The car-parkers tried to banish me to the service entrance, and when

I insisted I was an invited guest, they simply looked the other way. I had to park the truck myself up on a hill, discreetly out of sight.

We also had a listed phone number in a land where practically even the plumber had a private line. Teddy didn't work on movie charities and wasn't a member of the Junior League. She helped the nuns at school, and when there was time left over, joined a noble band of ladies from the church who spent afternoons visiting the sick and aged. I suppose there are Hollywood orgies, but we never made the guest list. For all intents and purposes, we were living in Indianapolis with palm trees. Occasionally some tourist would wander up the driveway with a map of movie star homes in his hand. "Is this the Hedy Lamar–Humphrey Bogart–Lauren . . . ?"

Just goes to show you how neighborhoods change.

What we didn't realize was that we'd changed too.

The first hint I had came from my publisher. He said with his proper Boston diffidence, "You know, of course, that we've never had a good author stay in Hollywood."

"Well, why is that?"

He fiddled with his Phi Beta Kappa key and then his hand moved in a vague ellipse out over the swimming pool. "Just . . . everything here."

I was puzzled. Everything here had been profitable, I felt. On the heels of *When the Bough Breaks,* I'd done another novel that was reprinted in a national magazine and won a book award. And I was cranking out television regularly enough to have a good income. I created pilot films, produced some shows and wrote many others. There was excitement in working the studios; the structure of the business made you feel wanted, important. The people were persuasive. Everything was a rush; you were always convinced that the cast, horses and Indians were stomping around waiting for the next page to spool through your typewriter. What you wrote was mucked up pretty badly when it hit the screen, but by then you'd been assuaged with a nice check and were onto something else that had even more promises attached. In fact, someplace in these busy writing years I sold the two original stories I'd written for the Americana TV series. The buyer was the same network that had said they'd be commercial

19

duds. My stories became the pilot films for the network's new series, which was almost an exact copy of the one that had moved me West.

Economically, television made sense. I could write a show in a couple of weeks and be paid more than the advance royalty on a novel which would take me at least a year.

Slowly, though, I did begin to understand what the publisher had meant. It was a surfeit of blessings, perhaps the kind of euphoria one gets in skydiving. You become so fascinated by the beauty of the unreal world you're falling through that you forget to pull the ripcord. And the danger in show business was believing it. Live long enough in a hall of mirrors, an echo chamber of enthusers, self-deceivers, you finally lose all reality. Further, if you wanted to succeed, you had to give it your life. The compulsively intense men who ran the business demanded no less. The "industry" was everything to them, they said, so why not to you? This meant dawn-to-dusk commitment, Saturdays, Sundays, long hours over drinks after the sound stages were dark. The work didn't bother me. It was the endless talk-demands, the reliving of filming, the totality of thought that excluded everything else. The commitment, I could see now, was a drug, and it frightened me.

I left studio employment then and came back to our hill. A writer could work any place, and in Hollywood many do work at home. The risk is, you're out of the swim. You don't bump into so-and-so at the studio commissary who'd hire you to do such-and-such. Hollywood, I'm sure, invented the phrase: out of sight, out of mind.

Another more subtle change was also taking place. I was nearing forty now, that spooky, unpredictable time when you realize you're no longer a boy: the options are pinching off. In the film business, I'd had more near-misses than an admiral at Midway. I'd written thousands of pages and cashed a lot of checks, but I still hadn't hit my big picture, the fame shot that you needed out there, or felt you did. It began to dawn on me that I was just not a natural dramatist. I've known Hollywood writers who for two or three hours, with infinite variations of plot, can talk a story that they make up as they go. They're in the oral tradition. They know the effect of a line. They hear. But I have to see and labor over plots.

Then, too, the writing of effective novels demands that you plumb into yourself, bleed the stuff out of your own misery. My background ranged from Princeton–war–suburbia to a glittery mercurial Hollywood. God knows, the show-business story had been done often enough; likewise suburbia, and I'd told my war stories. So, nearing forty, I began to wonder who I was, and what to do with my craft.

The answer came out of the world I began to see around me. I was struck by an increasing materialism and amorality in national life. As Faulkner said, "Something has happened to the American Dream. We dozed and it abandoned us, and in the vacuum no longer sound strong, loud voices, unafraid." The old values were dying and we seemed to be telling ourselves good riddance. I couldn't buy it. My God wasn't dead, and far from feeling guilt about my country, which was the popular syndrome, I felt I owed it a debt of gratitude.

So, on my hill, I wrote another book, did seven hundred pages about a land called Hedon. As I saw it, this was the Utopian end point toward which we were groping. Out of this draft, months later, came a slim little novel called *Good Friday, 1963*. It was a spiritual plea, a polemic that we return to our sense of individual responsibility that I felt was eroding.

Well, my timing was almost as bad as my title. The spiritual concept of the book was somehow translated into politics. Several senators snatched it up, and I was plucked at to make speeches, get on a soapbox. Meanwhile, the book managed to gain momentum and sell quite well. I received letters from all over the country, and some were very gratifying. Apparently other people were also searching. A judge wrote me from Florida that the book had changed his life.

It changed mine too. I felt I'd found a mission for my writing. There was an urgency; people seemed to be listening, and it was unthinkable to me to go back to some bland boy-meets-girl story or send more posses chasing bandits around a hill. My publishers warned me tactfully that if I kept writing in the same vein, I'd get tagged as an ideologue. Then Teddy became concerned. "You're allowing yourself," she said, "to be pulled away from fiction. It's not your job to propagandize. Just tell about the people. You can do that." Even the boys were bothered by my sense of gloom. Tom once said, "What's the point of us growing up,

21

Dad, if everything is as lousy as you say it is?" About then, in their wisdom, they dubbed me "Mr. Anti-World."

I suspect they were right. Without really knowing why, I found myself spending more and more time away from the humdrum of the city. I'd drive for hours to get to a lake and hunt ducks, or chase off down the lonely roads of Mexico. One day a producer with whom I'd often worked called me over to the studio. He was hiring me to do a pilot film on a new hour series; it demanded the usual rush, tension, excitement. "When can you start?" he asked. This was Friday, and I told him Monday. He frowned: why not immediately? I said I had to go out in the desert and look at some land, maybe hunt some quail. It was as incredible to the producer as if I'd said I was going to Mars. Nothing waited for a pilot assignment. Everybody was scrambling, scrounging, trying to get jobs like this. Why not me?

I kept asking myself the same question: Why not me? Why was it, I wondered, that the only peace I seemed to find was someplace out in the hills in the slow rhythm of nature? I'd always refueled this way, from the days of the peanut-butter commercials to now. I didn't want the structure of the corporation, regardless of whether its product was refrigerators or television shows. The chase for each seemed to grow ephemeral. You tried to win the game, make the most money because you were raised that way. I'm naturally competitive. I love to play games, and demand of myself winning. But out in the California hills, or on a beach or a mountain, the sounds of the crowd seemed to slip away, and the reward too.

Didn't matter, alone on the land.

Instinctually, I suppose, I began then to seek my escape. I thought: if I could get a little hideaway someplace, go to the world I felt comfortable in. I started reading the acreage ads in the papers. It became more important to me to talk to real estate men than producers. Sometimes I'd take the boys with me out to some god-awful dump out in the desert and on the way back they'd say, "Oh, Dad, you're never going to get us a ranch. Anyway, it's kind of a lot of bother, driving for hours on some freeway." That was the kids' way of saying: Forget it, brother, we'd rather stay around the hill and goof off with our friends.

I could hardly blame them. Kids demand continuity. Our home was a paradise and they were naturally rooting in to it. But the trouble was, our lofty isolation could only be part time. Daily the kids had to go down the hill to school, be with their friends; they belonged here too, and this was what bothered me. They were growing up in a city paved over by concrete, a massive traffic jam choking on its own exhaust. On certain hot fall afternoons their football practices would have to be canceled because of smog. In rush-hour traffic, for a kid to ride a bike any place was a death-defying gauntlet. In fact, there just wasn't time to be a kid, to be alone, to dream. Everybody's children were like little robots, it seemed to me, wound up and sent off on a frenzied schedule, hauled here and there by their station-wagon mothers, pushed, programmed, treated, tested. Worse, the kids seemed to accept this way of life as normalcy. When they had any time off, the temptation was to use it passively: lounge around a record store, or, on a beautiful Saturday afternoon, sit in a double-feature movie. It was the rare child who tried to amuse himself creatively. The milieu seemed to tell them that they were owed entertainment and instant gratification. In the Beverly Hills world—sleek, rootless, overstimulated and over-TV'd—you were handed your pleasures. You had no chance to make them yourself. Much as we might try to wall it out, the environment kept flooding in, and the kids, naturally—because they wanted to be like their friends—sopped it up.

Though Teddy and I loved our life on top of the hill, we also felt a fatigue. There was a sense of being pressed by mountains of details, lists, and appointments that didn't mean a damn. Somehow, the living had gone out of life. This fact didn't bother other people apparently, but it gnawed at us. In our social life, we never played the game to get to know the so-and-so's and help my work. We rarely had to do "business entertaining," the drudgery of most urban dwellers. But still, in any group of friends there seems to arise a definite form of social competition. So Teddy would spend all day running down to Beverly Hills in search of milk-fed veal, fixing flowers, cooking a superb dinner. We'd have a party of good friends, and when Teddy and I would pick up the ashtrays at one A.M., half hungover and talked out with small talk, we'd ask ourselves: What for? What's it all about?

More saddening was to watch old friends beginning to break up. One man would be a great success in business but his home life was a mess. Another couldn't handle booze; another, his kids.

And almost all seemed taut with inner problems. They existed on the stimulus of work, work, work, get to the top, make it. They lived for their business role and had little beyond. Like us, they couldn't slow down enough, get off the treadmill long enough, to find themselves and what they really wanted. But then, as I thought more about it, I realized this had been the case in any society we'd lived in. You didn't have palm trees in New York, you had soft sheltering oaks in suburbia, but the game was the same, regardless of where it was played. Pressure, money talk, chitchat, a rising din. And Teddy and I, apparently oddballs, kept asking ourselves: Is this all life is supposed to be? Where's the quiet growth of self, where's exuberance and going free?

But we never answered the question, until, gradually, Teddy began getting stomach pain. She's an organized, perfectionist girl, gives herself totally to any challenge. And was it the car pools or charity work or social life? Or me, lashing around trying to find which direction to go? Maybe all of it, but the diagnosis was specific. She had ulcers. Her face would get yellow-gray; she'd have to go to bed; and the annoyance of that would make her sicker still and she'd grow a second ulcer on the first.

We began then to take a hard look at ourselves. We had everything in our lives, all the diversions and richness that one of the most fascinating cities in the world could offer. What the devil was the matter with us? Well, as we saw it, we just had too much. We didn't seem to have the detachment to pull back. We kept kidding ourselves that we loved it, yet down deep we felt a creeping disenchantment. Something big was missing in our lives and we knew now we had to find it.

One afternoon, about then, I was called over to a studio. They were filming a script of mine, and the well-known star was also the owner of the show and the director. He said to me, and he was a legendary "good guy" in films, "Otis, I just don't like the ending."

I was puzzled. The ending seemed simple enough. His wife had cuckolded him, he would now mount his horse, and as she tried to cling to him, he would stroke her hair once, then wheel off and ride out of her life forever. "What don't you like about that?" I asked.

For two hours, while the horses and Indians were stomping around, we sat side by side in studio chairs. We had a highball.

We chatted pleasantly about many things, but never once did he give me a specific objection to the scene. Finally he got up to go to the men's room, and a wise old assistant director whispered to me, "Look, hasn't it dawned on you what the trouble is? He [the Star] is getting old. He's spreading out across the butt, therefore he don't mount horses very gracefully. Also, by having the wife clutching at his knee, you give her the last big closeup."

Star strolled back, and I said, "I think I've got it. You don't *mount* the horse. You just walk beside him and lead him out into the sunset."

He grinned in his famous way. "Perfect, Otis. We'll shoot it."

When I came home that night, I told Teddy we, by God, were going to take our own walk out into some sunset. We were going to get out of here for a few months over the kids' summer vacation. I wanted the boys to have the chance to slow down, know themselves, live in the woods and fields. To be sure, they could have plenty of outings on their own hill, but that wasn't the challenge I wanted for them. We needed a shared experience, I felt, a kind of peace that can only come when you put the city roar and the conformity of your peers far behind you. When you make it on your own as a family, the hard way, in a strange new land. And the danger was, we didn't have much time left. If all of us wanted to find some reality out beyond the L.A. Basin, we'd better grab it soon.

Through my various real estate peregrinations, I'd made a contact over in Utah. The next weekend I took Tom with me on the Union Pacific, and we seemed to go backward through time. We went up to the very same Wasatch mountains where years before on the train I'd first dreamed with the kids about getting a ranch. Only it wasn't that easy. When Tom and I rented a car in Salt Lake and drove east into the Uintah mountains, we hit a wild spring blizzard, highways blocked. The real estate man couldn't get to us, or we to him. In a little Utah town, we had to hole up in a motel. Couldn't even buy a drink in Mormon country; there was no movie or TV. Yet here, that night, I did get one of those inspirations books talk about but writers rarely have.

With the blizzard howling outside, I created a satire about a character named Sam Eagle. Sam was the "old America," a nineteenth-century man, trapped in a cave. When he was blown free by an atomic test shot, he came out into a world he'd never made;

he was used, abused, and, finally, in bewilderment, fled back to his cave.

Almost the moment I finished my outline, the phone rang in the motel room. It was the real estate broker saying he'd found us a really dandy little ranch. Only trouble was, "it's snowed up awful bad in where it lays. Looks like it's gonna be late spring before I could even show you it."

"I don't mind waiting," I said. Because, from what he'd told me, I had a hunch about the place. It sounded like I'd finally found my cave, to write Sam Eagle in.

People ask, "Just how do you go about getting a ranch?"

Patience. That's where you start, and then you proceed to forbearance and utter exhaustion. Most ranch real estate brokers I know are perfectly nice fellows who don't mind a ten-hour day in a car, and can talk for every minute of it. Regardless of age, they often call themselves "Old." Old Luke, Old Rafe. It's beguiling, farmy. They look the part: western boots and string ties; they can chatter cows but when you get down to the hard economics of running a ranch, ask a rancher, not a salesman. In fact, searching for ranches, you'll meet some of the dumbest or just plain lyingest folk in the world.

For years in California, I'd described to brokers exactly the kind of ranch I wanted. Instead of saying flatly they didn't have it, they'd drive me over endless washboard road to look at something the Joad family would have fled from. I'd say at first glance, "Not for me," but they wouldn't let me go. We had to tug open wire gates, climb up rocks, examine every withered blade of grass. And never would they tell you about the sleepers, the real reasons a ranch was on the market. In one place in California it was a nearby cement plant; you couldn't see it from the ranch but when the wind was right it would pour tons of noxious fumes over the "dream spread." But they only ran the plant once a week. Feller from the city could be sold the ranch, say, the day before, when the air was sparkling clear. Or, on another place, I found buried deep in the hills thirty trailers and shacks, a Hooverville subdivision. It was a big ranch; Old David Harum had just avoided showing me that little valley.

So I was on my guard the afternoon in May when Teddy and I bounced along in a pickup truck in northern Utah. We'd already been gone four hours from Salt Lake; then we got on a sheep trail through sand, rocks and washouts. Old Melvin, the thirty-year-old real estate man, was charming us with such country-isms as, "Phone, you say? Wal, there was a phone out here once, but do you know what happened? Them doggone bears chewed down the poles. There she's a-laying," and he grinned, pointing at a gnarled pole in the sagebrush that was so wormy and ancient, it had to be petrified wood.

As we drove up what he said was Rock Creek canyon, I got that familiar feeling. The road was a disaster, the loneliness overwhelming. For the third time in the last hour Old Melvin chuckled and said, "We's getting close now."

We came through a grove of aspen and into a small valley. There was a mine shaft, blasted out of a granite cliff, a scatter of old shacks, a rusted mine car, bedsprings and a 1930 auto body. A stream ran from the abandoned mine down into several large beaver ponds, trickling beyond through heavy grass to Rock Creek. On both sides the mountains rose up in sheer crags perhaps three thousand feet above the valley. There was no power, the phone line conquered by the bears; I could see one privy and about a hundred yards of fence, the rest rusted away. Old Melvin crawled stiffly out of the truck and beamed. "Now, ain't this something! Yessir, folks, this is a real showplace."

We went in the "house," which was a sagging shack, the boards creaking loose. Somebody had pried the lock off the front door, so we just pushed it open. On the kitchen table were fish bones, coffee still in the cups, cigarette butts and blue grease congealed on plates. "Them doggone hunters," Old Melvin said, "they sure didn't clean up last fall, did they?"

"Damn junk pile," I whispered to Teddy. "I wouldn't be caught dead here. Let's go."

She was looking beyond the shacks at the mountains. "I think," she said, "it's the most beautiful place I've ever seen. It'll be just right. Oh, darling, I hope we can buy it."

The argument that followed turned out to be the shortest I ever lost. Maybe it was sheer desperation after my searching in California, but finally, with Teddy prodding me, I did make the owner a cash offer.

He'd been trying to dump the place for a long time. But now that an outsider had come in and shown such feverish interest, the owner began to brood darkly. What did I know that he didn't? Maybe there was gold in that mine after all. When I told him I just wanted to run a few cattle, he bellowed, "Why, mister, any damn fool can see it ain't no cow place."

That did it. He was convinced I was trying to steal something. Only after much bickering did we finally agree to a tentative, narrow-eyed summer lease.

There were, however, several conditions. I was to fish sparingly; not damage the rocking chair which the owner swore had once belonged to Mark Twain; run poachers off, and accept Wells Robertson, who went with the place. Now, this Wells, the owner said, "would rather tell the truth on credit than lie for cash. Plumb honest, but he takes some knowing." Wells didn't happen to be around the first afternoon we saw the place. Apparently he lived in one of the shacks on a diet of peanut butter and carrots; he was there to mine gold and do some other strange things that he kept in his shack and even the owner had never been permitted to investigate. The owner didn't pay Wells anything, just let him squat in return for caretaking.

Though it was a sight-unseen hiring, Teddy said, "Perfect. We need somebody anyway . . ." and that way, and that unprepared, we began our pioneering.

In early June we drove up in our International Travelall, a neat little Good Life family from Beverly Hills. We were loaded with sleeping bags, fishing rods, dogs, kitchen supplies. This time, out strode Wells Robertson, a brush of stiff red-gray hair, the tall lank of him shambling toward us in his greasy overalls. He squinted at us, sniffed us. If we was coming in wanting to fish, there weren't none allowed. No, I said, we were just the renters. I thought maybe the owner had told him.

"He don't never get up here," Wells said. "Nobody does. Ain't no reason to except prowl around, make trouble of some kind."

The boys, by now, had exploded out of the International, leaping and yowling like long-caged monkeys. They wore Bermuda shorts; Peter had strapped on capguns. Bang—bang! They went splashing into the beaver ponds, out again to snatch old iron spokes and miners' buckets and start fencing with them. "As you might guess," I said quickly to Wells, "we're pretty much city people. What I want to do . . ." and I hurried on about buying some cattle, horses, teaching the kids what a ranch meant, how to fence and work.

Wells was grimly silent. He kept breaking an aspen stick into inch-long fragments, and when that was done, he held up a stub of one finger.

"A cow," he said, "bit me when I was doctoring her, as a boy, infection come, I lost the finger. So I ain't never enjoyed livestock.

Besides, season being short, I got mining to do, wouldn't hardly be time . . ."

"I was thinking about fifty dollars a week," I said. "And we board you, buy the food . . ." I almost started describing Teddy's cordon bleu cuisine.

"It ain't a matter of the money," he grunted. "Don't never need much in my line of work."

Then Wells said he had something to do, and drifted off toward his shack. As he stooped to go in the door, a yip from one of the kids held him. He stared at them, shoved up his leather cap and scratched his head. Eventually he sidled back to me. "This here notion," he murmured, "was kindly for me to . . . be in charge of them?"

"Exactly. I'd want you to work 'em, kick their tails if they don't mind you . . ."

"I believe it's a question of them listening, though. You take there"—he pointed over toward the boys—"that one swinging the ax, I have seen a feller cut his foot off like that, if you could have told him . . ."

"Tom!" I hollered. "Put that damn ax down. You're doing it all wrong."

"Aw, Dad!"

I sighed and looked at Wells. "That's why we're here."

He nodded. "I ain't been around kids much. Come from a big family but we all got scattered young, I off walking sheep mostly. Do know that one boy is a boy, two's a half, and three is no boy at all."

"I know it will challenge your patience," I said haltingly.

"Wal, I suppose I might could make a little free time. Ain't going no place else exactly. Mornings I could tend 'em, get 'em to cobble a few fences and such. Afternoons though, I'd want to myself. I'm digging"—he nodded vaguely toward the cliffs—"up in the red ledges. I wouldn't want nothing to interfere with that."

"Nothing will," I said, and had to grin. "Who knows, maybe we'll all strike it rich here."

We did, but in a way I'd never dreamed. It was the isolation, I suppose, that began to possess us and change us. In Beverly Hills we thought we'd been close to our kids, yet we always seemed to be rushing off, driving some child to a friend's house, or I had a tennis game or was working; appointments, urgencies and just plain nonsense plucking us apart.

Not on Rock Creek. Here, the togetherness was deafening. Nobody came, nobody called. The boys slept on the floor of a grimy shack, got up with the sun and went to bed soon after the northern twilight paled. For a while there was novelty enough to keep us all busy, but slowly a feeling of emptiness crept in. We were alone; we had to fill our days with our own things, find new resources within ourselves.

Well, a writer lives in a dream world anyway, and I certainly didn't suffer in this one. In the mornings I'd work at my typewriter; afternoons, I'd fish. Teddy would say, "I don't see how one man can possibly fish so much. Don't you ever get tired of it?"

A ridiculous question, deserving no answer; besides, we had a language barrier on the subject. What she'd see every afternoon was an otherwise normal human being slipping into wading shoes, taking a box of bird feathers and wandering off, to be stung by mosquitoes and drenched shivering. You can't explain madness like that, let alone count the hours on the grassy banks of the beaver ponds or the next bend of the stream you've got to try before you quit. Brooks, rainbows, browns, cutthroats, they were all here in profusion. Rock Creek was unpredictable, a fast hoyden stream. You never knew what to expect. On one familiar sandy bar I noticed a log that had apparently floated in. Just for the hell of it, I threw a Coachman at the log. I was standing not four feet from it. The fly sucked under in a swirl of current. There was a faint tug; I figured I'd probably snagged a branch. I snapped the fly out and cast again. The log was gone, thrashing in the middle of the stream, my rod screaming line. No fish ever had a shorter fight. When I horsed him, flopping, up on the sand, he looked like a Christmas stocking of red and gold coins. I smothered him with hands and knees, fought my fingers into his gills and held up a five-pound brown trout. I ran him across the stream, fell down, forgot my rod, raced the mile back to our cabin. We took his picture on a big flat board, with the kids grouped around. And Teddy had the temerity to ask me the next day if I was going fishing *again!*

Only reluctantly that summer would I pull myself away from the trout. As Teddy reminded me, we had to try to make the "ranch" pay for itself. Indeed, that was the hope, and it meant cattle. I packed the boys in the blue truck and we drove two hours to the nearest livestock auction barn. Up on the podium the auctioneer was chattering his selling banter, pound prices raising in dimes, quarters, fifty cents a hundredweight. I didn't understand his gibberish and hadn't the foggiest notion of how to get a bid in. I began winking at the auctioneer, raising a thumb the way I'd seen others do. Finally a local rancher took pity on me, said, "Mister, I'll buy for you. He's a-watching me." By then it was late in the sale and the cattle we ended up with were striped and spotted, cast-offs from dairies, tall, short, horned, unhorned. Fortunately, I didn't know how bad they were, and it was a proud moment when the boys and I went into the chutes and seared on our brand, $\frac{T}{O}$. Then we hired a rackety truck and took the refugees home.

Well, we had cattle; now we needed cowboys, duly mounted. Here, I was more experienced, having grown up around horses. Yet in buying them, nothing helps like luck, and I was amazed at ours. Out of all the potential broncs and spoiled cayuses, and from a horse trader who was just that, we managed to get four gems. "They're a mite old," the trader said, "but they're safe and they'll do you." Did they ever: God knows how many green kids and just plain indecencies later, three of those horses are still in our family; Smokey, Strawberry and Jamaica, plugging it out loyally, as they have from that very first summer.

When we got our string back up to Rock Creek, the next big job was learning how to use them. Wells hadn't, that I knew of, had anything bitten off by a horse, but he sure acted like it. He wouldn't go near them, so it was up to me to teach the boys to ride. Like all kids raised watching TV westerns, they felt you just got on a horse and pushed the go-button. I tried to make them understand that this hot rod was alive; he could feel things and you had to anticipate his feelings. You mustn't slop around, tease him, get him in any position where he'd be forced to act like a horse.

Sure, sure, Dad. All elbows and floppy knees, they knew everything in about a half hour. Finally, after several days of instruction, I told Teddy I'd done all I could. If somebody got a broken leg or worse, we were two hard hours from a doctor, and then only if you could catch him at his office. Faced with such a situation, you just had to put 'em in God's hands and pray.

What those horses suffered I'll never really know, but occasionally, I got some echoes. Because now the kids had erupted into full-blown TV cowboys. Tom even had the swagger, hat tilted over his eyes, thumbs hooked in his belt. They'd canter off crashing through the willows and aspen and disappear across the creek. This particular plot was known as searching for strays. They'd ride for miles in rocky, brushy country. I'd warned them to stay out of bogs, knowing from my fishing trips there were some treacherous old ponds near the creek. Tom went straight to them, like I'd given him a road map. His boots are still down there in the muck, and why he wasn't whacked by the flailing hooves of Jamaica is a miracle I'd just as soon forget. Another time John was galloping through timber, which he'd been forbidden to do. He found himself suddenly on the ground, knocked off by a low branch. Good old Smokey just stopped and waited for him to figure out the obviousness of that one. After the boys had exhausted their various dramas in the timber, they'd go down to an open stretch of country on the neighboring Ute Indian reservation. Here, they'd gallop flat out hour after hour, and we're still trying to break that habit in our three horses that have survived.

There's an old saying in the West that a horse won't hurt a kid, and that's the only explanation I know. Because ours got away with it somehow. They began learning how to put on saddles right and move cattle that invariably wanted to go the other way. Wells taught them fencing and how to chop firewood instead of feet. When he'd go off mining in the afternoons, the kids were left to their own amusements. Quickly they decided they weren't fishermen; leave that to the crazy Old Man. They made Huck Finn rafts, smashed them in the swift creek and emerged blue with cold. They read voraciously, and when they tired of it, they'd run footraces. Next they built hurdles and finally went on to pole-vaulting. They didn't know how to do it, so they cut aspen shafts and taught themselves, the climax of which was an Olympics they put on, with Teddy and me as the cheering section.

Peter, at this time, was going through a flute period; he'd wander out and serenade the horses, and when that didn't bedevil them enough, he'd get on bareback or backward, lie down on their kidneys or tickle until they'd have to buck, at least kick. He was so in love with the horses, he slept many nights with them out in the pasture.

Saturdays we'd drive to town for a bath, a movie, stay in a

motel and go to church on Sunday. Soon we made friends among the Utah people; the boys particularly were looking for "families with daughters," and they found some beauties. The Mormons, with their pure Anglo-Saxon strain, seemed invariably to breed fair-skinned girls with cheeks like apples. Once Tom and John were invited to a local ranch for haying. After a day's work in the "Church's field," Tom jumped on a horse bareback with one Mormon lass. Impishly, he thought he'd show her a Beverly Hills trick, popped her a kiss on the back of the neck. She whacked him off that horse, and no more surprised gentile ever stared up from God's tithed acres. Later the girl's brother stayed a week with us at Rock Creek. He was shy at first, our gentile world frighteningly new to him. Eventually, though, he seemed to accept us as a pretty decent lot until I'd pour a highball. He'd stare at the bottle with the white horse on it and finally he'd ask, "Mr. Carney, that is horse medicine you're a-drinking, ain't it? Couldn't be whiskey?"

But of all our transitions to the new life, the most startling was Teddy's. I had married, I thought, a delicate, feminine type. Now, dumped into a tiny rat-infested shack, she was positively thriving. Our bedroom was the size of the double bed and one foot more. The privy was way out someplace through thistles, cold and shivery at night. And for a refrigerator . . . that was a hundred yards away, the stope of the old mine shaft, which was ice-cold inside because of the stream of water that came out of the rocks. You had to put on rubber waders to slosh in and get your meat, bring it back and try to cook it on an ancient wood stove. For Teddy, who'd learned in civilization to be a superb cook, this meant an entirely new technique: synchronizing the boys' woodchopping, my lighting, stuffing in chunks of aspen, getting the damn thing too hot, then too cold, adjusting her recipes to work in seven-thousand-foot altitude. (She can't multiply hours by pounds even at sea level.) The stove was an ugly 1890 robot; it could bite and burn you, splatter, sizzle; you'd cuss it, stuff more chips in; then the pipe through the ceiling would start to redden; you'd put the roof fire out and go back to work. Yet Teddy not only wrestled the monster down but got the best of him, learned to have several foods coming to boil or brown at the same instant, with the hot water for washing dishes bubbling on the back of the stove. And that wasn't enough. She was determined to bake her own bread, cranking up the stove in the afternoons until the tiny kitchen was sweltering hot. I'd come in to see her face mottled red, her hair stringy. She'd jerk open the oven in a gasp of heat to pull out four swollen golden loaves. Next she bought a cow, milked morning and night in clouds of mosquitoes, and then went on to making cheese. "My God," I said, "if your mother could see you now."

Fortunately, nobody's mothers did see us, or I'm sure they would have tried to rescue us from such folly. Our grabbag cattle had begun to die with exotic diseases . . . not many, just enough to take any possible profit out of the scheme. Wells, good as his word, avoided cattle like the plague. There was no veterinary help available, so Teddy and the boys would be out in the meadow until dark, giving penicillin shots to a little steer they named Ferdinand. He was not meant to live, but when they lost him, everybody cried. Another time, Teddy, the boys and one of their friends cornered a steer in the wreckage that served as our barn. He had an infected horn they were trying to doctor; he kept charging back and forth across the barn, the kids trying to rope him or drop down on him from the eaves. Finally, when they got him cornered, he made a rush at them. The friend from Beverly Hills leaped out and cried, "Ungawa!"—the legendary Tarzan scream. The steer stopped in his tracks, astounded. They caught him, treated his horn and, miraculously, he lived.

If the economics of our "ranch" left something to be desired, I did feel that my writing was profiting by the experience. The peace and quiet seemed to stimulate me; when I got away from the typewriter in the afternoons, the hours spent chasing trout seemed to ready me for better work the next morning. My Sam Eagle character was rolling along nicely, and much of his thinking and dialogue was lifted straight from Wells.

Because when night would come, the bugs buzzing on the screens and the Coleman lamps turned up, we moved out of our time dimension and into the past. It was the only place to go, without phone, TV, radio or newspaper. We had two means of communication: music and talk. I had a ukulele, Tom, some drumsticks on a chair; Pete's flute, a piano organ for John, and for Wells, a harmonica that he hadn't played in years. I thought my songs were old until I heard Wells': "Red Wing," "Silver Threads Among the Gold," "Cowboy's Lament." What our repertoire lacked in numbers, it made up for in nostalgia. Invariably, after the musicale, Wells would begin to talk.

He was a shy, sensitive man. Like many hermits, he appeared laconic, even gruff, but this was just a screen of self-protection. Once he trusted you, he'd open up. You could walk away, go outside, he'd keep drawling on, as if now that he'd started the talk motor, he wanted to get his money's worth out of it.

Later I noticed him leafing through our books. He'd set two aside, Maritain and Sartre, wondered if he could have the borry of them. Help yourself, I said; it might be a long time before I got to those gentlemen. Wells read them quickly, and came back to give me a surprisingly accurate, if laborious, lecture on existentialism. It occurred to me then that he was like an old parchment volume; when you got the lock open and the dust blown off, you were amazed at the knowledge inside.

Wells' main forte was electricity. He'd been convinced for years that Steinmetz's original formula was wrong . . . not badly so, just a hair off, but enough to make all electricity suspect and, worse, wasteful. He'd been corresponding with General Electric for years now, trying to persuade them to study his experiment, in which the loss gap was closed. Because he'd only mumble guardedly about it, we didn't pay much attention. Then one day the kids stumbled into his shack to get an ax and discovered practically a warehouse full of wires, tubes, armatures and heavy steel magnetos. Wells was furious at the boys, padlocked the shack, and we dropped the "electric" from our conversations.

There were a few nights, however—fortunate ones for us—when Wells' old partners, Willie and Wally, would drop in. We'd hear a knock at the shack door and a high, squeaky voice: "Anybody-home?"

This was Willie Davis, pegging in like a wispy bandy-legged owl. He must have been eighty then, ice-blue eyes, tough as a pine knot. Willie had come into this wilderness, homesteaded and raised a fine family. Now, when most men his age were in retirement homes or dead, he was still out fencing or riding ten hours a day, whanging packhorses up into the high Uintahs with hunters and fishermen. He could barely write. He'd taught himself to read off can labels. He spelled rope like soap, because, dang it, they sounded the same.

Wally, his sidekick, hadn't been around as long as Willie, but still he could remember as a child lying on the roof of their homestead shack, watching the dust of settlers' wagons coming into the newly opened Uintah basin. When Wally went off to World War I, he was so thin the Army had to spend three months fattening him to get a uniform that would fit. As Wells would observe to the boys, "In them days life was hard on western farms."

But the real bond between Willie, Wally and Wells was that they were partners in the rocks. They had the gold bug.

It was a strange contrast. Here were men so frugal they'd anguish over the price of nails; their lives were the antithesis of materialism. If they struck their bonanza, they wouldn't know how to spend it. But perhaps, as I came to understand, they never considered having a fortune. The search was all that mattered.

For years they'd been prowling Rock Creek canyon, looking for a gold mine that had figured prominently in Utah history. Back in the early Mormon days, Brigham Young had wisely concluded it was easier to feed the Ute Indians than fight them. His benevolence paid off. The Utes offered to show the Mormons the richest source of gold they knew. Brigham Young appointed a representative, Caleb Rhodes; the Utes blindfolded him and took him on a long ride, the destination a secret. Repeatedly Rhodes came back with massive amounts of gold, some in pure ingot form. The angels atop the Mormon Temple in Salt Lake are reputed to be cast from his treasure. The agreement with the Utes was that when Rhodes died, so would the mine. No other man would ever be shown it.

But Rhodes' son was convinced he knew the location. Shortly after his father's death, he went alone by packhorse up Rock Creek canyon. When he didn't return, ranchers and homesteaders took up the search and found him in a cave, shot dead. It was this story that brought Wells from St. George, Utah, to settle on Rock Creek. Here he met a Ute named Wobbin, who'd been raised by Mormons, finally persuaded him to talk. Wobbin took Wells to a lonely cliff in the canyon and showed him a pictograph. It read: "*Oro hoy* . . . gold today," then gave the number of mules and miners that were heading from this point toward the vein. By the next morning, however, Wobbin was apparently guilt-stricken at revealing the tribal secret. He went out with an ax and defaced the pictograph so it could never be read again. Wells showed me the scar on the canyon wall.

Wells and the other old-timers knew, of course, that the Spaniards had done a lot of prospecting in Utah. The Rhodes mine, because of the cache of ingots, had obviously been one of the richest Spanish strikes. The question was whether the Utes had managed to obliterate it to keep white men out of their land. Wells suspected this was the case but stubbornly kept "visiting" with Indians. He finally stumbled on one old man who told him that when he was a boy, his father had buried his dead in red ledges along Rock Creek. As the old Indian had dug the graves, he found gold and silver ore, but had no use for it, so he cast it into bullets. When it came to identifying the specific red ledge, this old Ute got memory sickness, and left Wells with only a tantalizing clue.

Aided by Willie and Wally, when they could spare the time, Wells kept trudging Rock Creek canyon. A particular clump of pines began to look promising. They dug and uncovered bones of a burro, remains of a man. They couldn't identify him, but felt certain he was a Spaniard. They kept searching, moving farther south where the canyon widened. Here a sagebrush valley along the old road appeared to them an ideal site for Indian attack on Spanish ore trains. They dug in the valley, unearthed bones, packsaddles, fragments of helmets and minted Spanish coins, dated from the early 1700's.

They delivered these treasures to a museum in Salt Lake, then went back to work in earnest. By now, however, the story had grown and become crusted with lies: city miners were flocking out, using electronic detection instruments. Shafts were dug, such as the one on our ranch. Rock Creek was obviously mineralized, but nobody knew just how much.

Shortly before World War II, Willie was helping the Utes round up cattle. As they camped one night, an Indian showed him some strange-looking black rocks. They were scattered as if by an explosion all over the ridge; the Indian didn't know what they were, nor did Willie. The puzzling thing was that they affected the magnetism of Willie's compass. Only after World War II and the atomic bomb did Willie realize these rocks must have been high-grade uranium. He got the same Ute to take him back to the ridge again. Empty, not a rock in sight. Willie rode countless ridges for years after, and never found another.

Wells eventually narrowed his search to a particular red ledge just south of our ranch. He refused to take me to the site, but when my younger brother, Peter, came out to visit, Wells accepted his credentials. Pete was a geologist; he took his rock hammer and off they went. On their return that night, Pete told me, "I can't see any indication that this is a gold-bearing stratum. But do you know, that old man with just a wheelbarrow and a pick has moved a hundred tons of rock. He's changed the shape of the mountainside. I didn't have the heart to tell him that I think he's in the wrong place. He could make a strike, you know."

But they never did, Wells, Willie and Wally. They just kept searching. And somehow, their lonely optimism, courage, their touch of a forgotten past rubbed off on us all.

As the summer drew to an end, I could feel the change that had come over us as a family. For one thing, we knew what it was to be bone-tired. The books I'd lugged up with me were still unread; I just didn't have the energy at night to plow through them under a Coleman lamp. But what we did discover was that rare satisfaction you get when you have to make your own life, when all your energies must be used in providing necessities of food and shelter. We found a vigor and stimulation that the city man cannot know in his world of symbols and pushbutton ease. It made me wonder, in fact, whether man, after his ages of being forced to survive, could really adjust so quickly to his new bed of affluence. Perhaps, indeed, it was the tension of city life that left him so drained and unfulfilled. It's a different kind of exhaustion when you've tramped the mountains after a grouse and chopped wood to cook him on.

But when you've been living in the nineteenth century, it's a jolt to go back to the twentieth. I realized that soon after we returned to Beverly Hills. The life there folded over us again in its luxury and glitter of promise beyond. I completed Sam Eagle, but found that instead of a satire he was a curio, an anachronism from the summer we'd had. My publishers were amused but firm: just get back, they said tolerantly, to telling a good story without a message. Sam Eagle went in the file. I hoped I could make him work someday, but I didn't have any idea how.

\* \* \*

That winter Teddy and I reached a decision: we loved ranch life and wanted a place of our own. Unfortunately, our rented hideaway on Rock Creek was just not practical. The acreage was too small; you couldn't run enough cattle to pay the interest on the mortgage, let alone support yourself. Indeed, this was the problem in northern Utah. Long ago the Mormons had chopped up their land into small farms. I flew back often to our beloved Uintahs, trudged around in the snow to look at various prospects, but the answer was always the same: uneconomic. At that time, it appeared you needed a place that would carry about 150 mother cows to pay itself off. (Now, nine inflated years later, the magic number is at least twice that.)

By spring I'd given up finding anything in northern Utah, so I began widening my search out into other Rocky Mountain states. I'd rush off to see some ranch that sounded breath-taking in the ads, but when I got there and studied the place, there was always some good reason why it was for sale: too little water, too expensive to operate, or ugly country a coyote would starve in. I'd fly home in despair, study some more ranch ads, and a week or so later, take off on another search. The finale was a fifteen-hundred-mile trek into Montana, a ranch that seemed just perfect for us. Then the owner came out of his house after supper and said, "Sorry, fellers. I just changed my mind. I ain't a-gonna sell."

An old friend who was a rancher had taken me on this wild-goose chase, and now he gave me some advice. "You've got to get a good broker," he said, "and let his outfit do the legwork for you. Otherwise you'll spend years chasing around and never find anything."

With this pessimistic and honest appraisal, we rerented Rock Creek for a second summer. I didn't have the desire to write a book, let alone an idea for one. I began doing some scripts for a religious TV show; I read a lot and tried to enjoy Rock Creek. The freedom there seemed just a taste of what we could have, if we found our own ranch and could make it support itself. By now, too, word was getting around among our friends about our Utah experiment. Many of them were clearly envious, thought we were a little nuts but wished in a way they could try it themselves. Others, however, were already showing concern. As one old family friend wrote: "Admittedly, the idea is fine, exposing the children to the sort of life you must be leading. But there is, you know, a danger. Suppose they should get to like it? You surely wouldn't want them ending up as ranchers . . . ?"

Not much chance of that, I felt, because now, by August, the summer was spooling away. I'd almost given up on the dream. I'd gone driving off to look at a dreadful place in Wyoming; coming back, I got lost in the timber and didn't get home until nearly midnight. Then Teddy handed me a letter.

To my surprise, my rancher friend in Montana had given my name to a large, reputable real estate firm and told them what I was looking for. They were writing me direct, they said, because they'd run onto a brand-new listing up near Pinedale, Wyoming. The description they gave seemed intriguing and the price was reasonable. They wanted to know when I could come.

"Why not tomorrow?" Teddy said.

It seemed strange that near
Evanston, Wyoming, that night on
the Vistadome, I'd first thought about
a ranch. And now I'd come back to the
same country, driving north toward Pinedale.

Only God, I thought, could love the bleakness
He created out here. It was an expanse of buttes and
tawny sagebrush, rising and falling like waves in an
empty ocean. This is the view of Wyoming most people
get on the Interstate highway and the Union Pacific; and
that's a pity. Because just below the buttes lies Fort Bridger,
one of the earliest pioneer settlements in the Rockies. Its museum has some rare treasures from an era that was too busy to
save many. Nearby, scattered in mournful sagebrush draws, are
ghost towns like Opal; during the Union Pacific construction
days, these were brawling tent cities, later becoming shipping
points for massive migrations of range cattle. Buffalo herds
crossing the rails here would delay a train a half a day. To the
north, the empty barrens were the main route of the Oregon
Trail. In some areas wagon ruts can still be seen. Old-timers tell
that in their youth, when they drove the trail, they were literally
down in a trench. It was cut that deep. Even now, jeeps with
electronic gear ride the ruts and pick up bullets, guns, pots and
pans that jostled off the wagons.

As we beat our blue truck up the road that afternoon, the kids
were with us, and after four hours of travel were getting antsy.
John said, "I bet you, Dad, this ranch isn't going to be any good.
Just like all the others."

"Probably. Say, look out there: that's the Green River. It goes
through the ranch."

Pete sniffed. "I'd rather have Rock Creek."

We were now in a grove of cottonwoods along the river,
where the Green breaks up into smaller channels. I knew the
spot because I'd passed it before. I was Names Hill. Thousands
of covered wagons had forded the river here, and on the far side,
wet, thankful emigrants carved their names in the cliff. You can
still read some, dates in the 1840's, with Jim Bridger's name
prominent.

The road got emptier then, and straighter. We hardly passed

a car. But I'd expected this. Once, years before in my first dream of ranches, I was so naïve that I didn't even know how you started to look, so I wrote the Chamber of Commerce in Evanston. They put me in touch with a broker, who recommended a small ranch south of Pinedale. Well, I had no idea of the distance involved. We drove with him this same road, two hundred and fifty miles north of Salt Lake. And worse, in late April it was blustery, snowing. We had looked at a couple of bleak places near Pinedale and, south, at Big Piney. I felt like I'd just been to the Arctic Circle. "My God," I said to Teddy, "I'd go stir-crazy out in this loneliness." We didn't even spend the night, turned in terror and fled home.

But now perhaps we were different. In the July sun, the storefronts and boardwalks of Big Piney glinted with a kind of stubborn defiance, out in the vast plains and hay meadows that made up some of the largest ranches in Sublette County. This was the contrast with Utah: there was an openness here, a "see farther and see less" freedom that appealed to me. Driving, we passed occasional cowhands, leathery and slouched, riding beside the road. They'd nod at you, but you had the feeling they didn't see many strangers.

Then, to the east, the Wind River mountains began to rise, and the Bridger Wilderness within them. The range was a massive upthrust of granite battlements, turrets, and three peaks rising over 13,000 feet, the highest in the state. Even in July there were still patches of snow on the mountains; the streams we passed over were crystal-clear and flooding out onto the hay meadows. This area, I knew, rarely went dry. Locked in that spine of mountains, which was over a hundred miles long, were uncounted thousands of lakes. Behind them were ancient glaciers; only on a few hot days would they melt enough to release insects frozen here millennia ago. It was a savage stronghold, so formidable that there were still places humans hadn't set foot on, and the interior had never been surveyed into sections, only mapped by air. Tucked into the west slope were the lakes and streams that created the headwaters of the Green. "The ranch must lie up there," I said to Teddy. I was pointing toward great bald escarpments which were called by such names as Battleship, Sheep Mountain, Sawtooth, Faith, Hope, and Charity. Their ice-scraped gray cliffs sheared down to timberline. Here armies of lodgepole pine marched into shadowy canyons, forming basin after basin, then softening into pale aspen forests clustered on the lower slopes. These trailed off into russet willow loops which meandered along the Green.

The pavement ended at the log post office and store of Cora, which had been named after a pioneer cowgirl. The real estate broker from Denver was waiting for us. He was a young fellow in a city suit, carried a briefcase and called himself Mister. I could see we'd drastically changed our real estate type.

Through a friend, I'd turned up the name of one rancher in the Pinedale area. As luck had it, his ranch lay along the dirt road we were traveling, and we found him walking out of his hay meadow, wearing irrigating boots and carrying a shovel. When I asked him about the Ted Dew ranch, he said, "Hell, I didn't even know they were selling. That's a good little place. You better grab it."

As we drove on, I glanced at Teddy and crossed my fingers, then asked the real estate man how long the ranch had been on the market.

"Only a couple of weeks. We did put an ad in the *Wall Street Journal* and we've got about twenty-five replies. But you're the first people to see it."

I crossed my other fingers and we continued, eighteen miles north from Cora. Though the road was washboarded dirt, it seemed like a highway compared to the one at Rock Creek. And the country was superb: green rich grass, pocks of water, streams. We lifted over a crest, and in the valley below, with the river snaking through it, lay the ranch.

The main house, along the bank of the river, had been built by the original homesteader, and was covered now with asphalt siding that had worn thin. Surrounding it was a cluster of log buildings, shed, corrals. In the front yard stood a bandsaw and a stack of new-cut pine poles. There were elk and moose horns hanging on the fences, and cowhides out drying. What the head-quarters lacked in beauty, it made up in practicality. This, I knew, was a working place. These people were ranchers.

The Dew family came out then—Ted, his wife Elizabeth, or Dibs, as they called her, and their son, young Ted. We were introduced, and I noticed them glance at the Utah plate on our dusty Travelall. I was wearing my dirty Rock Creek clothes, a floppy black hat; the kids looked like refugees and Teddy wore a faded denim skirt and laced-up boots. The Dews must have been crestfallen. Here they'd listed their ranch with a high-powered firm and the first customers they got were obviously Utah hay hands, tire-kickers who, from the look of them, couldn't afford a motel room let alone a 2340-acre ranch.

But if the Dews had any doubts, they didn't show them. They drove us around with the broker, answered every question fully and honestly. The ranch had been their home for years. In the hard, wild land here they'd made a remarkably rewarding life. Until four years before, they didn't have electricity. They said goodbye to their friends in November, stocked up for winter, and came out again the end of May. Once a week they'd snowshoe to the mailbox, a three-mile round trip, to get the Calvert correspondence school lessons. Elizabeth Dew had taught her daughter and son in their living room. Because they had no schoolmates, she invented them; she created an imaginary "class" that called her Mrs. Dew; she asked questions of empty chairs and put her own kids successfully through the grades and into college. The Dews' reason for selling was that Ted had hurt his back, went through a disk operation, and was finding it increasingly hard to do the heavy work required. In fact, that afternoon as Dibs Dew described to Teddy the life they'd had on the ranch, her eyes filled up. She didn't want to leave, but they knew they must.

In talking with the Dews, I was struck by their weatherbeaten Wyoming independence. It seemed a different quality than even the rugged Utah people had. It was the bigness of these mountains and the isolated challenge of life here. For instance, trying to estimate ranch costs, I asked Ted how much beef he slaughtered each year to feed his family. "I never kill my own brand," he answered. That left a pretty hungry outfit, I thought, until he added, "Don't seem to make sense killing a beef you can sell, when you got all the wild game you need.'' Tom, meanwhile, was trying to befriend the Dew son, Teddy. He was a few years older than Tom, smoking a cigarette and sizing up the city kid. When conversation lagged, Tom said nervously, "Say, does your horse like apples?"

Teddy Dew squinted at him. "I don't know. If I ever had an apple, I'd eat it myself."

Ulp.

The Dew family had come into northwest Wyoming in a covered wagon. Theodore Roosevelt Dew was the youngest of many brothers. They settled first in the Gros Ventre region; then, after being crowded by neighbors, they moved up to this basin of the Green, the Black Butte area. They took up homesteads and bought others. Soon they controlled the valley. In addition to their cattle herds, they built the cabins for a dude ranch and ran it successfully for years. Ted, in his youth, learned to be an accomplished trapper. He'd snowshoe the creek and beaver ponds in the spring, set his lines, camp out. He preferred trapping to ranching in those days. But it didn't pay much, and to supplement his income, he'd gone to work for Bert and Ed Hill. They were the original homesteaders of the ranch, irascible bachelors who'd come up from Colorado and settled here. At the time of the Meeker Massacre in Colorado, the Ute uprising of 1878, Billy Hill, Bert and Ed's brother, had ridden in a posse that attacked Chief Colorow's camp. Billy Hill ended up with Colorow's drinking cup. He later gave this to Ted Dew, and finally the Hill brothers sold Ted the homesteads, which became his ranch.

As I drove around with Ted, I tried to sweep the place in, but, greenhorn as I was, much of it escaped me. The lower part of the ranch lay along the river bottoms of the Green. Ted pointed to one big loop of willows that was almost an island and said, "We call that the Moose Pasture." I thought he was kidding until he added, "We run 'em here practically like cows. You might say they're about half nuisance." I didn't know what that meant either until I learned that the winter before, Ted had been charged by a moose. He stepped outside his house to do the chores; a yearling bull came around the corner, struck him, knocked him down and tromped on him until Ted was unconscious. The only thing that saved him was his dog; when the moose attacked it, Ted got his senses back and managed to crawl into the house. Ted was alone at the ranch at the time, his head cut and with a bad concussion. "Well," I asked, "did you call a doctor? What did you do?"

"Wasn't much I could. Dibs happened to be gone, wasn't anybody here. I'd kind of lost my sense of directions, fumbled around looking for a handkerchief to stop the blood, finally stuck an old sock in my cap, went out and finished the chores." Then

Ted grinned. "When I came back, though," he said," I did call the game warden. I told him, 'The next moose that gets tough, do you just want me to shoot him and dress him out?' The game warden sort of chuckled and said, 'That'd be fine with me. I'll come up and get the meat.' "

On the lower part of the ranch were the hay meadows, about 315 acres that were dished in places with buffalo wallows. "This whole valley," Ted said, "was prime hunting ground for many Indian tribes: that's one reason why the country settled so late. The Indians took charge of it after the fur traders pulled out. It wasn't right hospitable around here for a white man. They didn't even get surveying this land until 1892."

Ted and the Hill brothers had worked hard on the meadows, leveled the land, dug ditches with horses and Martin ditchers. The ranch had the first water right on Boulder Creek, which spilled down from the Wind River mountains looming above us. "The first right," Ted said, "means you can take the whole ditch of water. We don't measure up here. There's enough for everybody, and I never have seen this place go dry."

But you got it on one end and paid for it on the other, Ted added. The winters were long and severe. Temperature went down to forty below at times, snow ranged from three to five feet deep. "How do the cattle get by?" I asked.

Ted grinned. "They just go into them willows and hump up. They can tell a storm coming a day before I can."

Apparently, if you fed the cattle—and it was a seven-day-a-week job—they'd survive without much trouble. "It's one reason the feeders like these cattle from up here," he added. "The climate pretty well culls out the weak ones, and the ones you do sell get fat for the man that buys 'em. I will say this about the winter, though. Once I went back to Minnesota and like to froze to death. Here it's dry. Sun out a lot. If you try to pitch hay with a coat on, you'll end up sweating most of the time."

The cows, he said, took two tons of hay apiece over the winter. This meant that the capacity of the ranch, as it lay now, was 155 cows. "We're a little longer on pasture than on hay," Ted said. "I have had as many as three hundred cows up on the pastures."

Then we crossed the old ranch bridge over the Green and drove north into the sagebrush. Out here we came over a rise and saw about thirty antelope in a band. They were less than a quarter of a mile from the truck, wobbly-legged fawns, a few bucks, their rump hair stiffening white in the warning signal. But they didn't run off; they watched us. Then Ted slowed and we hit a deep pair of ruts in the heavy grass. "Is that another road?" I asked.

Ted grinned. "Been here before the ranch, I reckon. That's a branch of the Oregon Trail. The Union Pass Cutoff, they called it. They came around those mountains above the headwaters of the Green"—he pointed northeast—"so they wouldn't have to ford the Green. Came right across the ranch here and out to the West Coast. People have picked up oxen shoes in these ruts."

We lifted up then into fairly steep rolling hills, and in a few minutes, came into a high valley, a crest of black lodgepole-pine timber and rolling swales of aspen. This was the upper part of the place, the summer pastures. "We call it the Castek Field," Ted said. "Old Man Castek homesteaded up here, built a cabin. When he died we moved his cabin down. It's the log bunkhouse you saw at the ranch."

This great basin seemed wonderfully isolated—six feet of snow in the winter, altitude 9500 feet, a game paradise: bear, elk, ruffed grouse. The black timber was echoing, menacing, as we drove on to look at Ted's cows. In the tawny afternoon they were lying in pockets of aspen, calves at their sides. "These cows will be good to anybody that owns 'em," Ted said. "They have been to us." Then we walked to the edge of a canyon; there was a stream here, Wagenfuhrer Creek, winding slowly down to the Green. The sides of the canyon were littered with aspen, felled by the beaver to make dams. Glittering in black descending steps were about a dozen beautiful ponds, and as I watched they were pocked with rises. I was supposed to be interested in cows, not fish, but I couldn't control myself now. "You have some trout, I see?"

Ted grinned. "There ain't exactly a shortage."

On the way back we passed two moose standing on an island in the river not fifty feet from the ranch house. Then, in the kitchen, we found Dibs Dew had fixed a salmon loaf, assuming we'd stay for supper, which we did. By now all formality was gone. I said simply that the place looked right for us and I'd like to buy it.

"Well, it's for sale," Ted said. "We tried to put a fair price on it. Probably sounds high. Everything's high these days."

"I'm not going to haggle with you. I think the price is fair, and you're entitled to it."

That night Teddy and I hardly talked at all. We both knew. We came back in the morning, and in the sun in the kitchen, on the Dews' typewriter, the real estate broker from Denver typed an agreement. It spelled out the cattle, the equipment down to the individual shop tools. I didn't have an idea of all the little devices there were on that ranch, scattered through the dark shop buildings. I didn't know a tractor from a Travelall. But the Dews did. They could have cleaned house on me, as green as I was . . . and beware, ranch buyer, this can happen, and does. But every item on our crude list, plus dozens we'd forgot to mention, showed up on our final deal. The Dews were that kind of people.

Because they were starting to hay, we left Tom behind, age fifteen, to "learn the business." Ted smiled. "Don't worry about him. I've broken in a lot of boys. Fact is, I'd rather have a good kid who don't know nothing than a wino who thinks he knows it all."

I wrote a check for a down payment, set October 1 as the closing date. As we drove away, Teddy and I glanced at each other. "Good God," I said, "we've got a ranch!"

In the golden autumn we came back to Wyoming. It was even more beautiful than I'd remembered; and ours.

We'd been fortunate in finding an excellent foreman, Dave Shannon and his wife, Mike. They were natives in the country, reliable, competent cow people. With their four children, they moved into the Dews' house. By now the Dews had bought a house of their own on the main street of Pinedale, and Teddy and I stayed around the corner from them in a motel, spending all our days at the ranch. I'd also brought Wells Robertson from Utah to start some carpentry work. Wells arrived in a truck with our loyal horses and Teddy's milk cow, Brunhilde. Wells pondered the country for a few days and said, "I can see now it's a more severe climate than I'm used to or care for. There is also no minerals to speak of. But I'll help you along for a bit, as I said. Then I'm going back to work on Rock Creek."

Next arrivals were my brother Peter and his wife, Marina. Pete killed an antelope and we had superb steaks. We floated the river and caught fish there and in the ponds. Walking along the pines in the Upper Place, my bird dogs put up grouse and sage hens. Then we shot ducks and geese. They're here in profusion. This is their breeding ground, and the local people hardly hunt them at all. "If a feller is going to spend money for ammunition," said an old-timer, "he's better off killing an elk or moose and having meat for winter."

I was, I thought, as close to heaven as I deserved to be. But there were some practical considerations, too. I now had a business to operate, and money seemed to be leaking out every place. We had to buy more cows to enlarge the herd into a practical unit. Dave Shannon had some good ideas about new ditches, new lands to irrigate. Further, the old ranch bridge had to be rebuilt. Ted Dew and some neighbors volunteered their help, and with Dave they did the job in the middle of winter, working on the ice, rebuilding the entire ninety-foot span so strong you could, as they said, "run a freight train across it." In the process, we dumped a bulldozer through the ice, but the neighbors pulled it out. Everything, finally, got done. That was the slow, patient way business moved in the country, and I was going to have to learn it.

For instance, one glaring improvement that the ranch seemed to call for was, as they put it, "being hooked up." The lower part of the ranch was separated from the upper part by a strip of forties—forty-acre plots. The owner of these was also an old-time rancher. Ted had talked to him for years about a trade that would make our land contiguous and give him a better pasture, plus water and aspen shade for his cattle. It seemed so terribly logical that I hurried right down to see the rancher.

He was out in his meadows, digging hay for his cows. The city boy bustled in and without a moment's hesitation said, Look, here's what I want to do, we take this, you get that . . . No answer. The rancher kept breaking hay bales apart as if he hadn't heard me. When I asked him again, he finally muttered, "I can't see that the proposition would do me any good. It's been like this for so long, won't hurt none to leave it."

On the way back, I shook my head. It was so obvious: he was getting the best of the trade by far. But Dave, driving with me, pointed out my error. I'd been too quick. I hadn't sat down and done any visiting with the man. Maybe it wouldn't have changed his mind, but it would have warmed him up to the idea.

Nothing here was done in a hurry. Western hospitality had been around a lot longer than I had, and it seemed to demand that, unlike the city, you talk about everything in the world first, and business, in a kind of offhand way, last. The city man is decisive. He has to be. Here God and the weather do the deciding. The average rancher never likes to plan for the future. He just lets it happen.

Next order of business was a house for us to live in on the ranch, so before we left that fall, Teddy and I started drawing plans. We'd found a wonderful site, a high bluff overlooking an oxbow of the river. There was a ring of stones still on the bluff where the Indians had made a sweathouse; then they'd plunge down into the icy water. In digging our basement, we found charred sagebrush from some of their old tent fires.

The house we outlined was to be Spartan-simple, an unlovely little box. Nearby, however, and directly above the river was a site we were reserving for a bigger house. Someday, we said, God knows with what for money, we'd build it, and the kids and our guests could have the smaller place.

But we were starting from scratch, we soon learned. The closest architect was 120 miles away, the nearest large supply of building materials, Salt Lake. All right, we'd worry about that later. What about power, phone, water? The Dews had gotten electricity only as far as the ranch house. Now we'd have to extend the cables across the river to our new site. By a stroke of bad luck we were out riding for cattle the day the power company crew arrived. Landscaping, anyone? Apparently they'd never heard the word. After bridging the river with an overlength span, they put two monstrous poles right on top of the bluff in the center of what would be our living-room window. It took me two years to get them to move the poles down the bank, where now we can see only their ugly tops. The phone company agreed to hook onto the power poles, but they warned there were already seven families on the party line. It might seem a little crowded to us.

As for water, we were fifty feet above the main source of the Colorado but we didn't have a right to tap into it, and wouldn't anyway. Ted said we could go twenty feet down and get an "Indian well," but the water mightn't be clean or taste like much.

51

Finally the husband of the storekeeper at Cora came out. "I'm a witcher," he said, "I'll find it."

He took a welding rod in his hands and started to walk and weave. It looked like a dance of the Druids. Pete, my geologist brother, was giving him a fishy eye, until the witcher grinned. "All right, walk the rod over here yourself." Pete did, and the metal twisted so in his hands he could barely hold on. "I don't believe it," Pete said. "Show me the well."

"Drill it."

The only well-driller around the country was "feeling poorly," his wife said. Translate that to read, he had a slight liquid problem and it wasn't water. His wife called him by his last name, Moon. "Moon will be out, though," she said. But the well rig was too heavy to cross our bridge. We had to guide it about ten miles the long way around through sagebrush, and when it arrived, who began pounding posts for the guy wires but Mrs. Moon. She could sling a helluva sledgehammer, that lady. Moon, himself, never appeared until the last day, when at 230 feet, an eruption, a Vesuvius of artesian water, blew so hard we couldn't even case it to the bottom of the hole. Moon came blinking out in the sunlight, sniffed the water and said, "She's got a little sulphur to her, but she'll never quit you, I swear you that."

Never has, and Pete still doesn't believe it.

By now Teddy and I had had several weeks of rather furious effort. We shipped the calves and yearlings off to the market in Omaha. We said goodbye to the Shannons and went back to Beverly Hills.

We'd scarcely left Wyoming when we began to long for it. We were filled with the challenge of building a new life. Before we even got home, we decided that though Beverly Hills had been good to us, we had now outlived it. Tom was in his second year at Hotchkiss in Connecticut; the next fall John would go off to Portsmouth Priory in Rhode Island. That would leave only Pete at home. Because of a reversal reading problem, he'd always had trouble with school. But perhaps if he were in a simple country school like Pinedale, he'd grow in so many other ways that his bookwork wouldn't matter.

So we set the next summer, 1964, as the target date. When we arrived in Beverly Hills, Teddy called our devoted friend and real estate agent. "Leila, we want to put the house on the market."

"Oh, dear, you can't be serious."

"We are. We're going to move to the ranch."

"Well, all right," Leila said, "we'll get out a listing. If you're really sure."

When Teddy hung up, we looked at each other in a kind of terror. It seemed like such a tremendous leap. Did we have the guts to do it?

The truth was, neither of us knew. We'd fallen in love with Wyoming. We'd acted first, and then when we began to think about it, Teddy said, "It'll probably take at least a year to sell this house. Maybe by then the boys will be used to the idea. After all, it's going to be a real uprooting for them. This is home."

A magical word—"home." Family, career, background, all wrapped into one. You ought to be able to cut loose and get out. But you can't. It took us a year and a half of upheaval to understand how far we yet had to go.

On a gray drizzly day that
December, Tom came back from
Hotchkiss for Christmas vacation.
When we met him at the Los Angeles
airport, he seemed quite drawn, thin. Well,
he admitted, he and a couple of upperclass-
men had sneaked into a bar in New York and on
an empty stomach had belted down some Manhat-
tans. "I puked a lot on the flight."

"Don't use that word."

"I was sick, then."

"How's school?"

"Awful. I'm number seventy-five in a class of seventy-six."

"Oh, poor Tom," Teddy said. "You get into bed when we get
home."

Tom loves games. All our boys do. So that next day he, John
and Pete went down to play touch football with some of their pals
in Beverly Hills. They played hard and long. When Tom came
home he looked grisly, had a splitting headache, and we put him
back in bed. We thought it was the flu. There was a lot around.
By the next morning he was still running a fever, so we took him
down to the clinic. I was working at my desk that afternoon when
the phone rang. The doctor was one of my best friends in California. "Otis," he said, "I can't believe it, but this boy's blood
count is not right."

I knew him well enough to know his voice was tense. "What
do you mean?"

"Let's hope it's a bleeding ulcer."

"An ulcer? For God's sake, Bill. He's only fifteen."

"I'd rather have it that than something else. Bring him down
in the morning for a test."

From Teddy, I knew the barium routine, and now we saw a
carbon copy. Tom had a badly bleeding ulcer.

Why? we asked ourselves. What cause? A competitive boy in
a fine school, but he was poorly prepared; he just hadn't caught
on. Homesick? Or maybe he was too much like Teddy, demanding too much of himself. I thought of the tennis court on our hill.
There was a big bulge in the fence where Tom, from childhood
on, had banged his baseball bat into it. Reason: because he'd only
hit a single. He hadn't knocked one over the fence.

54

Teddy and I were both grief-stricken and guilty, too. Was it the idea of selling the house, leaving for the ranch?

"Oh no, Dad," Tom said. But later: "I still wish, kind of, that we could live here some of the time, and there some of the time."

"What about you, John?" I asked.

John shrugged. "I'm ready for anything. Besides, I'll be off to school. Won't be around here much."

"Pete?"

The hang-loose kid, Pete: "School is school. I don't care if I'm here or there."

To Teddy, later, I said, "They don't want to sell the house. It's perfectly obvious."

"But you want to get out of here. We both do."

And so I went back to sit in the study and look at the soft green California hills. Which way to go?

Fortunately, I didn't have to decide. In trying to line up tutors for Tom's convalescence, in showing the house to a constant stream of lookers, Teddy wore down. I insisted she go to the doctor. Diagnosis: "A new ulcer now. It's not as bad as Tom's, but she has a lot of scar tissue."

We then went to a specialist. He sat us down and said, "When I want to find an assistant, I look for an ulcer type. Because they're people who can do the job for you. They're the best workers. The trouble is, they can't turn it off."

In the discussion that followed, it was his opinion that Tom at his age, and Teddy with her history, could not control their ulcers any other way but through a vagus nerve operation.

We were stunned. We needed time to think, but events set in motion were snowballing now. With such an uncertain future, we knew we couldn't leave Beverly Hills. We took the house off the market. We'd stay an indeterminate time, try to cure Teddy and Tom without an operation. When Tom began feeling better, I spent hours with him, talked what I hoped was common sense, a philosophy. I tried to persuade him he didn't have to hit the home run every time. And Teddy didn't have to keep the best house, raise the best kids, and operate a ranch too. Couldn't they see that the results really didn't matter? As one doctor told them, "Who do you think you are, God? That the day isn't going to run without your efforts?"

Tom was at a low ebb, keenly felt his failure in withdrawing

55

from Hotchkiss. John, meanwhile, was a fine student, attending Loyola, a big city Catholic high school, for the last year before he went East. Tom wanted very much to go to Loyola too; his friends were there. We finally persuaded Loyola to take him, beginning the next fall.

If we were personally uncertain then, at least we had a lot of company. The world seemed to be going to hell in a basket. First, Kennedy assassinated; then a coup d'état and more assassinations in Vietnam.

About this time I happened to meet a French woman who'd just returned from Saigon. She'd watched the overthrow of the Diem government; indeed, she'd been with President Diem and Counselor Nhu the night before they were killed. The story she told seemed unbelievable at first, but it fascinated me. She was a world-famous expert in a black art known as psychopolitical warfare: the use of incidents, riots and inflaming the populace through the media as a weapon of revolution. She'd written the NATO manual on the subject. In great detail, she outlined how psychopolitical warfare had been used to destroy Diem, with the assistance of the United States. She predicted then, in November, 1963, that we had created a vacuum of power in Vietnam; we'd see successive governments of generals, all of which would fail, and finally, we'd be forced to intervene with massive commitments of American troops in a war we couldn't win.

Based on what she'd told me, and further research, I began a novel. I called it *The Paper Bullet,* shifted the locale to Central America, for I felt more familiar there. If psychopolitical warfare was destined to be a new force in the world, I hoped to understand it and dramatize it. My publishers seemed interested in the idea, but Teddy was wary. She didn't want to see me pulled again into a topical subject. She felt I needed to slow down, away from the fickleness of political events, and find truly who I was and what I wanted to write. The ranch ought to be an ideal place to do it; we had a business to learn, a new way of life. After all, as we told ourselves, once we got to Wyoming, the world pretty well stopped at the fence of the Bar E Bar.

We'd kept that brand, which had belonged to the Dew family since their homesteading days. It was known to buyers, and we seared it into the calves in a muddy corral in June. The neighbors turned out in force. This is the custom in the country: you help them and they do the same for you. They'd rope a calf, drag him in; Tom, John and Pete would pounce on him, rassle him down in the manure. They learned how to hold a calf, hamstring him behind and kneel on his neck. Then while one was branding, another would apply dehorning paste, castrate the bulls, pill the ones with scours (a form of dysentery), give shots for blackleg, rednose and brucellosis to the heifers. It wouldn't take three minutes before the little squalling calf was up, wobbling free, hurt so bad in so many places he didn't know where to scratch. Looks cruel, and is cruel, but nobody has ever seemed to invent a better way.

Dave then took over the boys. Gone was Utah and the cap-guns. This was work here, their own land, and sometimes they cussed it and Dave too. He believed in doing things the right way, and that was just fine with me, so the kids would learn. They cut timber, shaved poles, built fence, dug ditches; they cowboyed for hours in rain and hail, learned how to doctor cattle. Their sched-ule was rigid; they'd work in the mornings and get some after-noons off. As they learned, the pace of work on a ranch is not hard, but it's sure steady. There's always something that needs doing.

How our cowboys made it through that first summer, I'll never know. Tom, pounding posts one day, took a Herculean swing with the eighteen-pound maul, missed and almost got Dave's head. Another time Dave was fixing a tie rod under the truck. He told Tom to move the truck just an inch. Tom bucked the clutch and almost ran over him. One afternoon in July we were moving some cattle when a violent lightning and hailstorm swept across us. We were way out in the sagebrush, no shelter in sight. We had to cower under our horses' bellies, they leaping, whirling, trying to run from the pelting stones and near flashes of lightning. Dave happened to look up and saw Tom squatting calmly beside the barbed-wire fence. "For Christ's sake, Tom," he bellowed, "get away from that fence!"

A few days later he showed the kids a section of forty feet of fence where the top wire was gone, disintegrated. Lightning had done that. It'll run a fence for miles. Because of the thin air here in the altitude, lightning is a constant enemy. In the pioneer accounts, more people seemed to be killed by it than by Indians.

Once, in a noon storm, a ball of lightning crashed through the ranch-house screen door and blew up on the stove. Young Teddy Dew was working for us that summer, and the bolt went right past his face as he sat at the kitchen table. Fortunately, a moment before, he'd just pulled back his chair and put down his knife and fork.

As the summer drew on, Dave and I chuckled about the kids. "That Tom," he said, "sure starts fresh every day. Forgets everything you taught him the day before. But I will say, he's a helluva worker. And John is coming on good with the tractors. He's got a lot of machinery sense. Pete? Right now he just likes to play cowboy with the horses. We'll give him plenty of chance."

In August we went into another new world, that compulsive, dawn-to-dusk purgatory known as haying. We had five tractors to put the kids on, an old wooden stacker, tall as a house, known as a "Beaver Slide." The Dews didn't believe in baling; too expensive, and the hay, which Ted stacked expertly, kept better stacked loose. Over the years Ted had built many log cribs; they resembled twenty-foot-square forts dotting the meadows. They were about eight feet high on the sides to prevent the moose from pulling the stacks apart. The haying process, as the boys learned, went like this: Young Teddy Dew would mow. Sandy Shannon, Dave and Mike's oldest girl, raked the hay into windrows, with our John driving a second smaller rake to pick up the leavings. Dave drove the sweep, a tractor with bars protruding from it that picked up the windrows of hay in big mounds and dumped them onto a wooden platform on the Beaver Slide. Then Dave would dismount, run another tractor horizontal out from the Beaver Slide. This had a cable attached that would slowly creak up the hay platform about thirty feet in the air and dump it into the crib, where Tom and Pete were standing by with pitchforks. They'd shuffle the hay into corners that shed rain and snow properly, stomp and spread it around the stack. In between times, I heard, one would hide in the hay and the other would probe for him with the pitchfork.

Frankly, I was afraid to look out in the meadows. Our kids had never run tractors before. The meadows are crisscrossed with hidden irrigation ditches, and if you hit one going too fast, the tractor flips over backward on top of you. In the farm country papers, you read of such needless deaths every year. Meanwhile,

Mike Shannon was back in the house fixing three meals a day for the crew. They'd come in dirty, hungry, have an exact hour for lunch and return to the meadows again, working generally until eight o'clock at night. And what was most tiring about the haying was the feeling of rush. In a land where we have a thirty-day growing season, August is an awfully short month. Clouds build over the mountains, thunderstorms wetting the hay. I've seen snow in August too. So you hurry time, work Saturdays, Sundays. The towns seem to go ghost during haying. You can't get anybody on the phone. It's a month or more of man fighting nature.

But for all their basic incompetence, the boys did superbly. The challenge of haying appealed to them. "Next year, Dad," they said, "we'll have a lot of our friends come up. You can hire them and we'll really cut into this old stuff."

Well, we thought we'd had quite a few friends this first summer. We were delighted to have my brothers and sister and many of their kids coming out to the ranch. Then, to our surprise, we found all sorts of old friends and sometimes surprisingly new ones dropping by. The world is filled with fishermen, I guess, and frankly, I love to have them. I'll drop a typewriter at the sniff of a trout fly. But the problem was, we were all jammed together in our finally built little box house. Three bedrooms and a living-dining room where Teddy and I slept. Teddy had hired a lovely young Chinese girl from Hong Kong who was a medical student at UCLA. Mother's helper. Well, Mother needed help with all the troops she was feeding. And the Chinese girl added particular charm to the family because she happened to have a superb voice, loved to sing. John would get on our electric piano, mindless of the keys that didn't work, Tom would beat the drums, Pete peep his clarinet, and the little house would fairly shake. It jutted up lonely in the sagebrush, not a tree or shrub or blade of grass around it. We couldn't get doors for the longest time, so we hung blankets over the openings, lived pretty much like Okies. To landscape the house, Teddy and I did go up into the timber and dig out some young pines. It was backbreaking effort, lugging them and their root earth for miles in the truck. Invariably they'd die. As one local man observed, "Seems like, if God had intended trees to be on this bluff, they'd be a-growing here."

But at least now, after Utah, Teddy did have an electric stove and a refrigerator. However, planning meals for so many was a new challenge. It would take two hours for a round trip into town to get groceries, and because none of us wanted, or could leave the ranch, to go to town, we'd stock up Sundays when we had to go in for church. Teddy would buy by the gross and we'd be lugging case goods in like coolies. But many little hardware details, such as a hinge or a doorknob, often never seemed to be in the stores. Many of the local merchants were awfully slow-paced. After Teddy had gone to town four times looking for a standard curtain rod, the hardware man finally said, "Wal now, by gosh, I'll send a postcard down to Salt Lake and see what's happened." It never occurred to him to telephone. Teddy used to keep a list of details that needed immediate attention; a year later, when half of them hadn't arrived, she'd just throw the list away.

So it was a big leap from Beverly Hills, and we realized it more all the time. But the kids seemed to be profiting by it. I completed most of *The Paper Bullet,* John left to start his prep-school career, and the summer ended too soon.

I felt confident now that I could run the ranch and write there. In fact, it seemed to be just the ingredient that was missing in my life. But still the problem was: how did you live in both worlds? By now I'd learned enough about the cattle business to realize it was no bonanza. We had a fine small ranch, our expenses weren't staggering, yet the price of calves never seemed to pay them all. The cold fact was that I still needed, or felt I did, the security blanket of the film industry. The income I could make writing for TV was just the cushion I had to have. There was no other answer for us except to stay in Beverly Hills some of the time.

I was, however, getting to be a forgotten man in television. "You're a hard sale," my agent said. "You're never around when somebody wants to hire you. And when you are here, you're always working on a book, or don't like the ideas I bring you."

For Teddy, too, there was a readjustment and a helluva lot of work every time we came home. To pay for our ranching escape, we'd been renting our "Movie Star View Estate" in the summers. And the renters slowly were kicking it apart. They didn't have to kick hard. The house was never well built; now it needed painting, new roof gutters; a jungle of underbrush was growing up and the fire insurance people demanded that we start thinning it out. We had learned, in showing the house, that the sleek Beverly

Hills trade considered it quaintly old-fashioned.

Teddy, though, would get right to work cleaning and scrubbing. We'd always find some of the things we wanted had been left in Wyoming, and vice versa. "It would be so simple," she'd sigh, "just to have one house and never see another renter."

There were a lot of things that seemed simple that fall and winter, but weren't. The Presidential elections lay ahead and I was hired to work on a campaign. I wrote films and commercials for national TV; the weeks swept by in backbiting, intrigue and a kind of hysteria. When the election was done, I came away soured. I went back and finished *The Paper Bullet,* did revisions the publishers suggested, and then began to look around for some nice innocuous book that wouldn't try to save any worlds.

Because of my concern with Peter's reading problem—a neurological dysfunction that appeared to be very common—I began to work on a non-fiction book in the medical field. Everybody felt happier about that, including my publisher. But the rub was, I hadn't written medical stuff since my reporting and magazine days. Though I knew that the neurological field needed explanation to many parents, I began to boggle at the research involved. And frankly, I was amazed at the bitterness and polarization in medical circles. Good God, I thought, this is worse than politics.

But nonetheless I was proceeding come spring of 1965. And in the California sun, the world brightened. Teddy and Tom had managed to dodge being operated on. Tom was raising hell at Loyola, not doing much in the line of work, but at least he wasn't sick. John was happy and productive at Portsmouth, and Pete was rocking along nicely and playing his clarinet. Now that the dust was settling a bit, Teddy and I seemed to be getting a perspective. "I think," she said, "we probably do need both of these worlds. There's certainly stimulation here in Beverly Hills, after the ranch. Maybe we ought to accept our double life and start being practical about it."

Out of this conversation came a new idea. Because the house hadn't sold, and obviously needed repairs, we decided to remodel it into a rental property that we hoped would pay for itself in the long run. We knew, for instance, that the Beverly Hills trade shuddered at our tiny master bathroom, wanted a big, plushy one. Put it in, marble sink and all. Build a new foyer with a brick

61

floor, parquet some of the others. Convert an unused bedroom into an office for me. And make the place renter-proof by adding a large locking closet where we could store our better possessions, so we could move in and out with less wear on Teddy. Also, because our gardening service usually goofed off while we were gone, we'd install an automated sprinkling system that would irrigate our simplified garden night and day, by the clock. It all seemed to make sense.

An architect drew plans; we fell in love with them, and I began to sweat. Then the cost estimates came in; we cut, scrounged, and all the time I was measuring those dollars against the difficulty of bleeding them out of a typewriter. In the book field it takes a long time to get your money. *The Paper Bullet* was still dragging through copy reading, wouldn't be out for months, for they'd already set publication date back once. So I pecked away on the medical tome and in the afternoons began lugging barrels and furniture out to the garage, where we'd store them. By late May we'd stripped the house for remodeling. I loaded the blue truck and got us ready to go again to Wyoming. Teddy had been painstakingly wrapping all her glasses and china. She looked as tired as a cleaning woman at Las Vegas after convention weekend.

On the last afternoon before we were to leave Beverly Hills, I walked out of the empty house and collapsed by the pool. I didn't read or work, just sat staring at the live oaks. In the new landscaping plan, everything was going to be changed, a *fait accompli* now, and frankly, I preferred to turn my back on it. The next morning I'd be on the road to Wyoming, and things always got better then.

I dozed, until a growl from my bird dogs waked me. In the pale sun haze, there was a sudden halation. A car was thrumming slowly up the driveway. The dogs ran out barking; obviously these were strangers, because we didn't know anybody who drove a long sleek avocado-green Lincoln Continental. This, I thought, is all I need. Some damn lost tourist with a map of movie-star homes in his hand.

I called the dogs back and went slowly toward the car. Two young men got out. I'd expected the usual star-gazer types, lapelless coats, sandals, cameras. But these fellows were dressed in funereal conservative suits and carried leather dispatch cases. I'd never seen them before. For all I knew they could be FBI. One dangled his hand up out of the bite range of the dogs and waved tentatively. "Mr. Carney . . . Otis?"

"Yes."

They smiled. "We tried to call but your phone has been disconnected. We just took a chance on catching you before you left town. We're from Qualis."

"Who?"

They smiled again. "That's a production company at 20th Century Fox. We wondered if you had a minute . . . ?"

"Well sure, come in. We haven't got any furniture though, place is a mess."

"That's all right. We won't stay long."

They didn't. A half hour covered it. They asked me to create a new western TV series, and film it on the land where it happened. "As a matter of fact," they said, smiling, "you might even think about shooting it right on your ranch in Wyoming. That's why we want you, because you know what the frontier must have been like."

After they'd gone, I fairly soared out to Teddy. She was in the kitchen, never even heard the callers. Her hair was stringy, she was barefoot, wrapping and crating; it was hardly the setting for euphoria, but mine couldn't wait. Up until now we'd been gambling on living in both of these worlds. But here, suddenly, we could have our cake and eat it: the challenge of creating an authentic western in Hollywood, the calm writing of books at the ranch . . . and no worry any more about financing either. I almost began counting the royalties on the new series, and transferring them over to pay for the ranch.

Teddy rejoiced with me for a while, but then went back to the really important things, packing her boxes. I poured a drink and walked out on the terrace. As I looked at the pale smog haze and heard the throb of traffic on Benedict Canyon, I had to ask: How come? What made the angels decide to drop in this particular afternoon? If they'd arrived at the same time tomorrow, they would have found us six hours up the road to Wyoming. They would have hired somebody else, and the settling of our worlds would have passed us by. I had to chuckle at the irony:

20th Century Fox, buying our commuting ticket back to the nine-teenth.

It was beginning to have a magical feel to it, like a night in New Jersey, with Teddy falling down a staircase into a new life.

At nine-thirty the next morning
I was sitting in Bill Self's office at
20th Century. Bill was head of television for the studio, and I knew him to be
one of the fairest, most successful men in
the industry. Moreover, the executives of
Qualis, producers of the show, were decent, ar-
ticulate fellows. They'd had good backgrounds in
advertising agencies. Though this was their first network television show, they seemed to have all the right
instincts about it. Qualis meant quality, and we were going
to do a western that was true to the reality of the frontier. I'd
been waiting a long time for an opportunity like this.

The germ of the idea, Bill Self explained, had been submitted
to the American Broadcasting Company by Fox. ABC had been
whetted by a brief outline; they wanted to see more. Basically, it
was the story of a family named Monroe. About 1880 the Monroes
left Illinois in a covered wagon to homestead in the West. Their
original destination had been Oregon, but now that I was in the
picture, we'd settle them down in Wyoming. There were five kids
in the family, the oldest boy, Clayt, being the main character. My
first job, through some acceptable device, was to kill off the
Monroe parents. Alone, then, the kids would be forced to survive
in a wilderness . . . and this was the gimmick of the show.

ABC felt it had a lot of warmth, the kind of family strip that
could go on for years. Furthermore, since Fox also produced *Peyton Place* for ABC, and programmed it as two half-hours weekly,
each ending in a cliff-hanger, they wanted the same programming style on the Monroes. "Peyton Place West," you might say.
But wholesome, no sex, just nature, animals and lovable kids in
peril.

My assignment—Bill smiled here—was to create the world
the Monroes would find. Portray the wilderness as it must have
been then, and sell it to men back in New York who wouldn't
know a homestead cabin from a Caesar Salad. I was to do this by
writing a novelette in which I'd set up all the characters and put
them in action in twenty-six episodes. The problem in any series
is to convince the network that you have enough story material.
Here, with five characters to play off, plus dozens of others I
would create, we felt sure we'd still be spinning our yarns long

after most network vice-presidents had passed on.

Then the Fox group wanted to know if I'd had any vibrations from the brief Monroe outline I'd read.

As a matter of fact I did, and had jotted down some thoughts the night before. These dealt mainly with eighteen-year-old Clayt, the hero. I read aloud from my notes: "Clayt's a kid who is torn by his responsibilities. Because he thinks and feels strongly, he should have some sort of dream he wants to pursue. Maybe it's medicine, government or the sea. But the point is, Clayt never gets to his dream, as many of us don't. It's always over the mountain."

They murmured agreement, and emboldened, I plunged on: "But someday, you know, we might let him reach it . . . and find to his astonishment that what he has on the ranch is better than the dream ever was. Perhaps this is his maturity."

They nodded again, but one executive frowned. "Maybe I didn't get that last part of it. You mentioned 'ranch.' I thought Clayt was a homesteader, log-cabin sort of thing . . ."

"You're absolutely right," I said. "Clayt's certainly no rancher. I guess I just flubbed the wrong word in there." Then we all smiled, shook hands, said what a great association it was going to be. As I went out the door they added, "Not trying to rush you, but we've got to get this novelette pretty damn quick, while they're still hot on it. You know how it is back in New York."

"I know how it is," I said.

A couple of hours later, the station wagon loaded with dogs, kids and fishing rods, we circled up the Benedict Canyon hill, out toward the desert and the mountains. I never felt happier in my life.

By the time we arrived at the ranch, I'd had two days of driving and a chance to put my thoughts into focus. The Beverly Hills world I'd left was still clear in my mind: it was an arena where you got up in the morning and clawed for the jugular vein of life: compete, earn, beat the other guy, get the job.

At the ranch, nobody cared. They never had, I guess. They'd always been too busy just surviving.

This was the great contrast, and my challenge now. To explain survival as I saw it in the life and people of Wyoming, and

66

then trace it back to its beginnings in pioneer families like the Monroes. I was going to have to interpret dour hard-bitten nineteenth-century values to an urban audience in the twentieth. I wished I had a portable TV camera so I could aim it at the ranch and play the sound and picture back in a network board room in New York. Better still, I ought to corral a half dozen of the gray-flannel-suit boys and trudge them around with me. Get mud and manure on their feet, get them cold, mosquito-bitten, make them live with people who'd never had time to worry about image or performance. For these Sublette County folk could always look you in the eye and tell you straight. If they got mad, they didn't hide it. If something was true, they said it whether it would hurt you or not. They didn't give a damn what the world thought; they were utterly themselves and proud of it. They rode out time like a bronc, confident that they could ride it down.

So first, in bringing the Monroes to life, I had a problem of feel. What was it like, this wilderness they came into? I knew I couldn't answer that question by helping Teddy and the kids unload our caravan. I pulled "writer's privilege" on them, and instead I just began to walk out along the bluff of the river, to stretch my legs and see this land with Monroe eyes.

In the oxbow of the river below our house, a beaver, still as a log, was drifting in the big trout pool. I tossed a pebble at him, and he banged his tail, slapped the water like a gunshot. You had to begin with the beaver, really, because if it hadn't been for him, the Monroes wouldn't have known this country existed.

The Green River had always been a paradise for the beaver, but it wasn't until the early 1800's that he began to have economic value. Beaver hats had become the fashion in Paris, London and New York. Lean, grizzled Yankees, French, British, Canadians and Scots trekked into this wilderness from St. Louis, camped along the banks of the river and began to gather hides. The trade was rich, and to the mountain men, worth the gamble it proved to be. For these headwaters of the Green were an ancient hunting ground of Shoshone, Blackfeet, Gros Ventres and Sioux. The Indians attacked again and again; there were massacres, vicious running battles and a few perilous escapes. But the stubborn mountain men kept fighting for the Green. Overland from St. Louis and sometimes in bull boats, they brought out wagons, jingled trade goods, beads, junk coins in front of the savages.

Soon barter began. The usual transaction saw the Indian stacking beaver pelts to the height of a long St. Louis rifle; the trader would give him the weapon for the hides.

Down the river from the north, and directly across our ranch, had come the Stuart party. John Stuart was a Scot, traveling with a band of trappers, engagés or assistants, and one half-breed woman. In Stuart's journal, he described the country and the river bluffs where I walked. He and his party had arrived here in August, starving. They came to a stream, Twin Creek . . . I could see the exact spot about a mile west: a willow thicket where Twin flows into the Green. Without telling Stuart, his men had drawn lots and selected a sickly old Canadian engagé. They'd kill him and eat him so the others could survive. When Stuart saw them aiming a musket at the man, he ran in and knocked it out of the executioner's hand. An argument followed, a mutiny beginning. At that moment, easing along in the sage, came an antelope buck. The trappers felled it with one shot, tore at the meat raw, and by the next day managed to trek on a few more miles west. Here they blundered onto a band of Shoshone Indians who supplied Stuart with enough food, and guides, to get him to Astoria, Oregon. He and his party became the first white men to cross the Rockies to the Pacific Coast.

As the fur trade grew along the Green, the trappers began great yearly gatherings known as the Rendezvous. Each summer, up and down these banks, they'd meet in camps that sometimes held a thousand Indians and whites. A few miles south of our ranch, the fur traders built a log fort called Bonneville. On a bluff nearby, Father deSmet said the first Mass in what is now Wyoming. But the tiny government of the United States was interested in more than prospering the fur trade. Our nation was locked in a power struggle with British, French and Spanish. The Rocky Mountains, Southwest, Northwest and Pacific Coast were at stake. Washington coveted these unknown lands, and it was the mountain men who explored them, becoming agents of state without portfolio. Out from the Green they began to prowl, on foot. Men like Jedediah Smith walked from here through Utah, New Mexico, Arizona, California, and up to what is now Oregon and Washington. Slowly their illiterate reports filtered back to Washington. They made crude but surprisingly accurate maps. Then, in a sudden whim of fashion, fur hats went out of style.

The beaver would be allowed to survive, but not their hunters. The old mountain men began to drift away; in their idleness they took more squaws and sired half-breeds. Many lay drunk in smoky hovels, and when they died the Indians buried them in rocky, unmarked graves. They'd been phased out of their livelihoods, their job done. Others, the youngsters like Bridger and Fitzpatrick, lived to see what they'd accomplished. Already the emigrants were starting west into the land the fur traders had pioneered. The younger mountain men became guides for the wagon trains. Manifest destiny, erupting on the banks of the Green, had opened a new nation.

When the fur trade died, the Indians moved into the basin with a vengeance. As Ted Dew had pointed out, they hunted it for so many years, and so jealously, that they delayed settlement of the entire area. Other places in the West homesteaded much earlier. But for the Monroes, or anyone, to want to pioneer in Sublette County took a good lot of courage. It wasn't until the 1870's that the first settlers came in around Big Piney. There was no survey of the land, so they just picked out creek bottoms and squatted. When the country was finally squared off into homesteads years later, the old-timers were mighty proud of what they'd carved out. One of them described the feeling to me. He leaned down, lifted a rock and said, "This is my rock, and that yonder is my tree. There ain't a goddamn man in the world ever gonna take 'em away from me."

As I walked, I looked up at the brooding mountains and the shadows of dark timber. Loneliness, that was what the Monroes must feel. When they arrived here, there would still be threatening Indians. Wandering hunters would appear at the homestead cabin, sometimes hundreds of them, with dogs, travois, squaws setting up tepees. They'd camp on the powerless homesteader; they were sullen, thieving, unpredictable. There are people in Sublette County who remember, as children, the horror of painted braves smashing into the cabin, banging pots off stoves; the kids would hide beneath trap doors, listening to the bare feet thumping above them.

If we were true to history, the Indians would be a menace to the Monroes for many years, and vice versa. I thought this as I walked north in the sagebrush. Just beyond the ranch line, I could see pine timber on the banks of a small creek. In 1895 several hundred Shoshones made a camp here and fanned out in hunting parties. Under treaty the Indians were allowed to kill game year-round. But already the hunting in this area was well known to sportsmen from the East Coast and royalty from England and Germany. The ranchers and outfitters in Jackson who'd guide the parties realized wild game was a valuable crop, and it was threatened now by what they considered careless slaughter by Indians. On a morning in 1895 a posse of enraged Jackson men surrounded the Shoshone camp, disarmed the bucks and led the prisoners down across our ranch. The historic route to Jackson, discovered by Stuart's party, follows the Hoback River. In this canyon, the Shoshones turned on the Jackson men. A few Indians still had their weapons. A running battle followed; there were casualties on both sides and many Indians escaped. The situation became so serious that the Army was called into Jackson, and troops remained there many months. As I'd written for the Americana series of TV, quoting from the history books, the frontier was supposed to have died at Wounded Knee, South Dakota, 1890. But five years later the corpse was still kicking up quite a storm, in the wild land where I now walked.

Threat. This was the dramatic grist I wanted to put into the story of the Monroes. I peered out at our hay meadows. White man had marked these bottom lands with his horses and his ditch-digging. But civilization was clearly a new kind of danger to the settler: more immigrants arriving and beginning to fight over the water and the richest, best lands. On the first survey map that Ted Dew had shown me, several buildings appeared in the meadows. No trace of them now, but one log hut was reputed to have been a saloon where some nameless homesteader was shot to death.

The last sun was gone; the stars had come out, and over the Wind Rivers a full moon began to rise, pale as ice, and so close here at the altitude of 7600 feet that you think you can reach out and touch it. I started back toward the house, shivered a little in the cold, or at the ghosts I'd been walking with. Four or five miles off, there were lights in a distant ranch house. Across the empty, rolling sage it looked like one of Remington's lonely scenes. On nights like these, strangers had often appeared at isolated ranches in Sublette County. The Butch Cassidy gang had used this wilderness as a hideout. They'd ride into a ranch, eight or ten grim-eyed men, a band of twenty horses, and announce they were going to stay a few months. There was no law here, nothing for the settler to do but board them, and, usually, they paid for the service. North of the ranch, up toward Union Pass, a local posse once pursued the Cassidy gang into the timber. A resident here, a boy then, had been riding at the point. The outlaws opened fire and shot off the tip of his thumb as he clung to the side of his horse. Cassidy rode on to be in somebody's movie, quite a different legend from the one known here.

In the moonlight, the distant timber was silver and resoundingly silent. It had been plundered too, but, like the beaver, had outlived its enemies. After the Indians passed, and the bandits, the lumberjacks came into these forests. We still find their cabins, sawdust and hand-wrought square nails. Their log booms lie rotting in backwaters of the river. Out of these mountains they cut the ties for the Union Pacific, floated them down to Green River City. They left their cemeteries along the banks. The headstones are cryptic. An occasional one will read: *Killed.* How? Another story I wouldn't have an answer to. But maybe that's a writer's role: to begin with truth and then re-create these people in the wilderness of the Monroes.

Several miles north, beyond our house, I caught a last glimpse of Dodge Butte. It juts up like a granite thumb in the forest; the moon lay shadows across its cliffs. Who was Mr. Dodge? Just one of them who had passed by. He'd shot a black bear up there, then his gun jammed and the wounded animal charged. The bear seized Dodge, clawed him, knocked away his rifle. When it tried to bite him, Dodge thrust his fist down the bear's throat, held it with claws ripping his face until the animal was choking, and Dodge knifed it to death. People remembered Dodge around the county. Because of the scars, he always wore a heavy beard and never took off his hat. And got his name on a rock before he died.

The more it changes, I thought, the more it's the same. Because the fall before, two friends of mine had been hunting just below Dodge Butte. In the noon sun they looked down into a big basin near the upper part of our ranch. They saw a large black animal partly hidden by willows along a creek. The only thing that size that would be out in broad daylight would be a moose.

But when they put field glasses on it, they sucked a sharp breath. Bear. An awfully big bear. We see quite a few blacks and browns, but never one this size. Grizzly? Taking their rifles they began to sneak closer. Then they were certain. A few grizzlies do drift in from Yellowstone, the bad bears that have gotten dangerous to tourists. The Park Service shoots them with a tranquilizer dart and dumps them far out in the wilderness. From the northwest corner of our ranch to Yellowstone is an uninhabited area, mountains, lakes, no roads, hundreds of square miles. So grizzlies occasionally wander through this, and the first civilization they come to is the ranches here. They've been known to kill livestock.

As the hunters crawled closer, the bear stood up, sniffed them. He began to amble toward the aspen timber. They fired— a long-shot, moving target. The bullet struck the bear in the leg. He began to bleed profusely and hurried toward the timber. But they knew they could follow him by the blood. They had horses to run him down.

At the edge of the timber he stopped. He took a swipe at the ground, caught some mud from a spring in his paw and plastered it on his leg wound. Then he hurried off into the timber.

There was no blood now. The hunters rode after him for several hours but never picked up his track. The next day I went back with them and we rode again, found nothing, except this remarkable lesson in brute wisdom. The bear had killed a cow elk. When the hunters had surprised him, he'd been carefully burying her carcass in the stream, covering it with willow branches so that the carcass would rot out, and he'd come back and eat it when it was ripe for his taste. His paw prints were still very clear in the mud. They reached, on my hand-to-elbow measurement, better than sixteen inches.

One day, I thought, the Monroes might meet a bear like him. What would they do if they stumbled alone and unarmed on such an adversary?

When I got back to the house, the lights were on, the fire burning. The place was a mess of suitcases, guitars, footballs, summer reading textbooks—baggage from another world. Teddy and the English girl who was her summer helper had already begun dinner. "Didn't you hear us calling you?" Teddy asked. "Where have you been?"

"Killing bears," I said, then drank a bourbon to it, because I knew now I had a start on my story of the Monroes.

In those last days of June the rains came and hailstorms pelted away the last traces of snow. The grass thrust up, and soon our neighbors began moving their cowherds across the ranch to summer pasture. Sometimes, at the noon hour, we'd picnic with them out in the sagebrush. Squatting around a pot of coffee, the talk would usually drift to the past. As I listened, the characters of the Monroes began to take shape.

Clayt could well resemble the young cowboys here: friendly in a laconic way, slow to judge people but hot-tempered if challenged; wise in this cow world and humbly naïve beyond it. Kathy, his sister, would have the land in her, like these women; she'd be as protective of livestock and animals as the children she'd later bear. The Monroe twin brothers, age about twelve, would be hellions. Such kids were known locally as a "riot and terror combined." I'd see them often at the Cora store buying fireworks, or sneaking beer at brandings. The Monroe baby, Amy, was still a question mark, but I figured I could invent some trouble for her along the way. For instance, she could become ill with fever. No doctor any place, try the home remedies, and after that—what? Well, I knew that the Indians built sweathouses; here, with a roaring fire and steam from the rocks, they'd sweat massively and then plunge into the icy water. Kill you or cure you. We might try that with Amy.

The people at Fox felt that since the Monroe family would be so obviously ill-equipped to brave the wilderness alone, they should have some sort of interpreter with them. I was duly warned that this was a tricky character. We didn't want a father figure or some protector who would shield the Monroes from peril. No, they'd have to suffer, but it would be nice if they had a friend from the native habitat to help them over the rough spots. The logical candidate would be a native, I thought, so I created a thieving but benevolent Indian named Dirty Jim. Fox liked the idea, but then word trickled back that New York was worried. Madison Avenue felt the race issue was awfully touchy. Couldn't I step around it somehow, give the Monroes some kindly old WASP character to play with? My answer was that I'd try to create an Indian that fit the time, let him grow on the audience for his own strengths, and the hell with the race issue.

A further instruction came up by phone call, and this one did bother me because it smacked of the familiar. Indeed, the studio admitted it had been lifted out of a Gregory Peck film. They wanted an additional conflict area. I was to create a cattle-baron figure, and pit him and his entourage against a slovenly nester family. The big against the little, and both camps hostile to the Monroes.

Fortunately, to counteract such a dreadful cliché, I did have some authentic models to work from. Sitting around with the cowboys after we moved cattle, I'd heard a lot of stories about a man named Abner Luman. He'd pioneered into Sublette County from Virginia and was a hard-bitten, remarkable gentleman. His cattle holdings ran from the Union Pacific main line some one hundred and forty miles north. He'd built this empire himself, employed hundreds of cowboys, and in many instances, had lent these men money to prove up on homesteads so they could go into business for themselves.

Luman was a leader, a benefactor, and a rough man. He'd ride with his cowboys in the long months of roundup. His iron discipline never wavered. Once, as they sat at a campfire on a sleeting April day, a spark from the fire popped onto Mr. Luman's greatcoat. He didn't see it, but the cowboys did. They were afraid to say anything. They watched the spark eat a hole in the coat. As they started to leave camp, Mr. Luman noticed the hole. He strode into an icy stream, sat down and drenched the cloth. When he stumped back out he kept striking his leg with his whip, repeating, "That'll teach you to burn your clothes, you stupid old sonofabitch . . ."

I'd also heard the story of a young cowboy going to work for Mr. Luman. It could have happened to Clayt Monroe. The first day the cowboy reported in, Mr. Luman pointed out the horse he wanted him to ride. After great difficulty, the cowboy caught the horse, a bad bronc. Mr. Luman told him to strap on a sack of potatoes and take them to the cook at the next line camp, some twenty miles away. The horse went off on the buck, the cowboy scattering potatoes the full length of his journey, then dismounting and carefully picking them up. When he finally limped into the line camp, the cook looked at him blankly and said, "Hell, kid, I don't need no potatoes. We got sacks of 'em."

When roundup was done, the cowboys came in off the desert, unshaven, stinking dirty . . . came to Rock Springs to ship the herd. Mr. Luman had a fine house here, and when the transcontinental trains would stop, Mrs. Luman would entertain friends and dignitaries. One time, according to the story, Mr. Luman strode into the house, followed by dozens of unkempt cowhands. A dinner party was in progress, fine linens, crystal. Mr. Luman said, "Mrs. Luman, get 'em up. Get 'em all up and out. Feed these boys. They're the ones that pay the bills."

Similar to Mr. Luman were other cattle tycoons in eastern Wyoming. Some of these were British shirttail royalty, remittance men, sent out to the frontier, where they built vast ranches, operated foreign syndicates that were cashing in on the gold in Wyoming beef. Out of such prototypes I created a character named Major Mapoy. And 20th Century Fox had their cattle baron, parentage unknown.

For the opponent, the hard-bitten raunchy nester family, there were parallels too, and close at hand: narrow-eyed mountain folk who raised their kids to hide under bridges, grab a leg of a calf or a lamb and pull him home to the hills. Such petty thieving has gone on in every part of the West, and it was born of necessity. In defense of the nesters, they were powerless against the cattle barons with their dozens of armed cowboys. One practice was to move a herd into a nester's ranch; custom said you could stay the night. By dawn the massive herd had wiped out all the nester's grass. He couldn't do anything about it except perhaps to sneak his brand on a few strays, to pay for the damage. The nesters were clannish, slovenly, proud; they knew how to live off the land, and some of them had indeed done this as border roughnecks during the Civil War. I named my clan the Wales Boys, and you could have found them in the hills of Virginia, or up along the Green.

With my people in place, I began the stories of the novelette. Twenty-six episodes or chapters, done in a continuing pattern, to be programmed, as I'd been told, as two half-hours a week. This meant that I was to leave the Monroes in peril at the end of each episode, somehow get them out of it, and into trouble again at the end of the next show. Occasionally, however, a particular chase or Indian war would take five or six chapters to resolve. In the beginning, getting the Monroe parents killed—I'd chosen drowning in the Green River because it seemed most historically accurate—this took one episode, and five more to introduce the Indian, Dirty Jim, and get the Monroes finally to the valley where they'd homestead.

Though the novelette strung out to 130 pages, the Monroe story was simple. It told most of all that the frontier was not as we know it on TV and film. It was years of boredom, loneliness; there were only rare moments of terror. But always the threat of them. I wanted to show the homesickness of a Kathy, watching endless rain on the cabin window, wondering if she could ever leave this place, get beyond the mountain. Or the powerlessness of a lonely Clayt against the violent, overwhelming wilderness. Fatigue, show this: that life was not sidling up to bars and having shoot-outs. You were just too damn tired. So the novelette was quiet, menacing and, I hoped, accurate to its era.

I drove to town and mailed it off. And then, with the ardor of estrangement, plunged back into our own real-life western on the ranch.

I'd gone down to the river to fish.
There was a good pool I knew. I'd
caught a three-pound brook trout in it
some days before, and now in the yellow
afternoon, with a brooding lightning storm
building over the mountains, I sniffed fish rising. Usually I float the river, but this time I
walked, out across the sagebrush to a loop of willows. There's a steep bank here, and with careful casting, you can get a fly to the riffles and the reverse current
beyond. The water just below me was black-deep and cold.

In addition to my rod, I'd taken a 20-gauge shotgun. I'd
noticed a badger up in this area and hoped to kill him. The
reason, simply, is that the badger digs large holes that you can't
see when you're galloping after calves in the sagebrush. If a
horse steps into one, he can break a leg or hurt his rider. Badgers,
ground squirrels and skunks are pretty much the extent of my
big-game hunting. Often, though, after seeing a dog come in with
a mouthful of quills, I debate adding porcupine to the list.

But this afternoon I didn't find the badger or anything else.
I set my shotgun down in the willows and moved slowly along the
steep bank, casting out into the river. Engrossed as I was, in
the whip of the fly and the constantly changing unknown of the
water, I never thought to look around at the bank, the heavy
jungles of willows. I imagined once or twice that I'd heard
branches rubbing in the wind.

Then I knew I'd heard something. I whirled.

A face was behind me, about fifteen feet back in the willows.
It was moving toward me, silently, a few inches at a time. I
sucked a sharp breath. The face was a moose we call Gladys. Her
big yellow teeth were bared, lips drooping down, and her hair
raised like knives on her shoulder hump.

I did a quick measurement. A couple of steps backward and
I'd be in the river. I couldn't run past her. About thirty feet to my
right, along the bank, I'd propped my empty shotgun in a willow.

I started toward it, a slow step first, then walking quicker.
The willows began to crash. Gladys came after me, flinging out
her big sharp hooves, her whole body sagging and grunting at
every angry step. I ran then, snatched up the gun, my fingers
fumbling into my pocket, dropping one shell into the river, get-

ting the other into the chamber, snapping it shut. Then I stopped and looked back. She was still about a dozen feet away, beginning to paw, her head low, ready to charge.

"Gladys!" I hollered. "Goddamn you!"

I didn't want to shoot her, and I wasn't too sure that one 20-gauge shell would do much good. Because this was a tough moose. The winter before, she'd attacked a cowboy at the neighboring ranch. She'd waited for him at night, when he walked out of the cookhouse to go to his trailer. After she'd charged him twice in a row, he hauled out a 12-gauge shotgun and shot her in the face. He blinded her in one eye, and that was how I recognized her. But the next morning she was still around. She attacked the cowboy when he was out feeding his cattle. He threw hay hooks into her side, and that drove her down to Dave Shannon, who was on his sleigh, feeding our cattle. At times Dave carries a rifle on the sleigh, but didn't have it then. Gladys charged him, knocked the team off the hard-packed snow trail, and they floundered in five-foot drifts, tangling in their harness. She took on Dave's cattle dogs, and finally drifted away. But right after we'd come to the ranch, she appeared outside our window one morning. She trotted around the house, stomped, peered in until we thought she was going to smash the windows. Maybe it's the reflection or just sheer cussedness, but moose have been known to charge houses too.

As this flashed through my mind, Gladys and I were locked in a stare-down on the bank of the river. I couldn't decide what to do. Then, behind her in the willows, I caught a glimpse of reddish brown—two ears. Four ears. They came wobbling out, her twin calves, big as Shetland ponies but not very old. I was aware that she'd seen them, exposing themselves, and now I knew that the moment had come. This was when she'd put me in the river. As she started toward me, grunting, I reached down, picked up a stick and flung it at her, then a rock, another stick. I kept hollering at her, backing away so I wouldn't have to shoot her. But I was running out of ground now. There was a steep bank I had to go up. When I got close enough to it, I turned tail and scampered up that bank. Gladys followed to the bottom and glowered at me. I threw some more stones at her, and finally she nudged her calves back into the willows. Then she stood defiantly in the center of my fishing hole, and I didn't go back down.

I left that piece of country to her, from then on.

If there was any foreshadowing in the incident—my being trapped and not knowing what to do—I didn't see it then. For we were having idyllic days on the ranch, that July. We'd get up about six-thirty, sun filling our little house, Teddy and I scrambling out of our bed, which, until it was folded away, took up most of our living-dining room. And there was always a houseful of kids, friends of the boys, up to work on the ranch. Breakfast was a bottomless horn of plenty down which Teddy stacked hotcakes, sausage, bacon, juices, eggs and toast. These kids never got filled up. Then they'd grab their leather gloves and hats, hurry out to meet Dave at eight A.M. and go to work.

I'd begin my stroll over to my office, an old trailer belonging to the Shannons. On the bridge, I'd always pause because the water was crystal-clear now, the run-off over. In the shadows beside the long pilings of the bridge, I'd visit a bit with my friends the trout. I'd tiptoe from one piling to the next: there'd be a big rainbow under the first one, then a brook, perhaps a cut-throat by the third. The water was sleek and slow. With fascination, I'd watch a particular insect floating toward me. If it was the right kind, and within a span of about four feet from where the trout lay, he'd dapple up and suck it down. If it was five feet out, he'd ignore it. There'd be another trolley along that he could catch with less effort. Sometimes, though, there'd be a particularly delectable morsel. The trout would scurry around, drift under the bridge and grab it with a slap of water. Then he'd wriggle back up into position and seemed to be delighted.

I was too. I'd identified the morsel as a blue dun; I could match it in my flybox when I drifted down the river in the afternoon.

Reluctantly I'd leave the bridge, walk the next quarter of a mile over to the ranch buildings. Dave and the boys were shaving fence posts and treating them in a barrel of preservative and diesel fuel. By now the mosquitoes were out, the kids slapping, everybody sweating a little. So Dave and I would sit on the stack of pine posts, have a smoke and talk about things on the ranch and a half dozen other subjects that didn't need talking about but were fascinating.

Finally conscience would overtake me. I'd go into the bleak little trailer, kill flies, and eventually confront the typewriter.

The trailer had a narrow hall, most of which was blocked by the typewriter, so I didn't have much choice. Oh yes, that book I was writing. Medical book. Non-fiction. At my feet was a large stack of dreary medical magazines, pamphlets; and out the window, the river with the rising fish and fields of sagebrush beyond.

Idyllic days. I got a rather plaintive letter from my publisher: How could I be writing a medical book and researching it properly up there in Wyoming? Answer: Very damn slowly. But I clunked along, put in my hours until the hunger bell rang. I'd flee back across the bridge, have a carnivorous, arms-groping-across-the-table lunch with the kids, then go outside and throw a baseball or football with them until they saw Dave starting the green truck and they'd take off on the run.

At that point I'd escape too, sometimes slipping down the bank, pulling out my tin boat—the *Big O,* the kids called it—and with my two-horse engine, putt upstream just far enough to find five or six good holes, fish them into the dusk. Or, other times, Teddy and I would catch a couple of horses, take off north in the sagebrush, then up into the black timber. We'd come over a rise and there'd be hundreds of antelope nooning in the grass. They'd get up, stiff-legged, and sniff us, then go bounding off. Or our horses would put up coveys of thundering big sage grouse; we'd see more moose; once Teddy and a girl she'd gone to school with flushed a nice black bear. The girl had a camera, so she and Teddy in their foolishness dismounted and followed the bear into the timber, calling to it and bravely brandishing the little sticks which were their armament.

But for hours, on our rides, Teddy and I would hardly speak. We'd ride through the cows and make note of sick ones or those that had died. If neighboring strays got in, we'd push them to a gate and over where they belonged. Most of the time, though, it was just quiet, long lazy afternoons, looking down on the beaver ponds, with the trout fanning in the pools. And we'd wonder if we weren't truly the luckiest people in the world.

In the evening the house would turn into a riot of noise and music from the kids. It seemed as if all their friends were musicians too. They'd lug in their guitars, whang away on ballads. And when finally everybody was hoarse, the kids would flop down and we'd just talk: bull sessions that seemed to go on for hours, and I treasured them. Here were kids aged from ten to, say, fifteen, city-raised. Maybe at home they didn't talk like they did up here; I don't know. Maybe there were always too many diversions and they never had a chance. We still had no TV or radio; there weren't many callers when you lived twenty-seven miles from town. So we just amused each other, spun yarns, and the bright eyes and goodness of these kids warmed me. I felt somehow I was father to them all.

They never seemed tired or wanted to go to bed. They were ablaze with ideas and dreams. Perhaps it's the altitude up here or the dryness that fills you with ergs of energy you never knew you had. Finally Teddy and I would pull out our Murphy bed and get into nightclothes. Sometimes we had to get into bed to convey to the kids that the witching hour had come. And long after our lights were out, we'd hear them back in their bunkrooms, the faint strumming of guitars and the chuckles at jokes or whatever it was that finally put us to sleep.

People ask: What do you do up there all the time? I guess you must read a lot.

In spells, when it rains or something like that. But most of the time when you can be outside in this world, you just drink it in and dream.

And the kids now had their dream too. One of their friends, Richard Correll, up with them, was a child actor from a show-business family. His father, Charley Correll, with Freeman Gosden, had created Amos and Andy and played them for years. Richard, bubbling over with talent, sold the boys an idea. We're here in the Real West, he said, why not make a western movie?

That was what they were chuckling about at night. They'd planned it back in Beverly Hills, lined up a 16mm-camera and begged or borrowed film. Then they asked for a few days off from work. They took the horses, dressed up with capguns and bandanas, and began their epic. The title: "It Really Matters."

The film was incredible. Stunts, falls, firecrackers placed in barrels of capguns, fired: zing, an invisible strand of monofilament fishing line would snap off a victim's cap, or another firecracker would explode in the dirt as a near-miss. Catsup blood would flow, and some kid would grovel, writhing, as he'd seen on TV. Poor Pete, being the youngest, was tied on the backs of horses, nearly choked. Tom was dragged on his belly through a specially prepared bed of manure. Richard, the young impresario, directed the film with consummate skill, then played his own stuntman. I watched him once make a run at our horse, Smokey, leap into the saddle, which turned belly under, and land on his back at Smokey's feet.

"Good God," I cried, "don't try that without the cinch tight."

"Mr. Carney," Richard said patiently, "that's the stunt, don't you see? I play a clown of a sheriff. He forgets to put the cinch on at all!"

Through it, loyal old Smokey stood like he was frozen into the ground, never twitched or took a false step. Hollywood paid a lot of money for horses like that.

But the first picture wasn't enough. After it had been declared a smash, the boys made a second, this time with a *girl* in it. And, in addition, a *real actress*. Frankly, Teddy and I had been a little dubious about this. Some old friends from Beverly Hills, John and Dorothy Swope, were coming up to the ranch with their daughter and son. The kids said, "I bet we can get 'em. They'd love to be in the picture."

Wait a minute. Dorothy Swope, better known as Dorothy McGuire, had just finished playing the Blessed Virgin in George Stevens' massive *Greatest Story Ever Told.* And John Swope didn't pose for many cameras. He was one of the finest still photographers in the country. But God bless the Swopes. Up they came into the middle of this madness. Dorothy produced her make-up kit; she'd even brought a western bonnet and gingham dress from some studio wardrobe department. And John put on a beard, got shot and stepped on in the first reel. Dorothy was beaten up in one of the numerous fights, shotgunned our Johnny in the stomach in a puff of baking soda and blew him out of a log cabin. We had sprained ankles, a wrenched back, a cut hand. I was shot dead in the first minute of action. I had one line: I rose up, dying, and whispered, "Rustlers. Save the ranch!" Along the way young Topo Swope was scripted to fall in love with Tom. He and Richard, playing the hired gun in black, did save the ranch. And when Tom, leading Jamaica, his mare, hesitated on a sunset hill in the sagebrush, Topo sidled up to him, wrung her hands. Her mother's line to Tom was: "Kiss her." Topo sidled closer, Tom scruffed his boots in the dirt. Then he leaned toward Topo, she melted to him . . . and Tom kissed his mare on the nose! Music up. The last long ride-out into the sunset, and the final title: "The Legend of Hairy West. The End."

Pretty much of a dream world for everybody. Hard to imagine there was anything else going on outside.

Then one morning in July, I was sitting over in the Shannons' house having coffee with Dave and several cowmen who were up looking after their stock. The talk was generally weather, beef prices and a few old stories thrown in. Then the phone began to ring. With all the parties on the line, it couldn't be for me.

Me?

"Otis . . . buddy!" a voice warmed when I picked up. Then there was a kind of awesome silence. "You have done it. They're in love with it! The whole package."

"The what?"

"The Monroes! What else!"

The cowboys at the table had their toothpicks out and were finishing their coffee and last cigarettes. I eased the phone around the corner of the room, because the century I was listening to, Beverly Hills, twentieth, just wasn't going to fit the one I was looking at. I pressed the phone to my ear so that the studio hyperbole wouldn't leak out and astound the cowboys.

But even knowing that this boundless enthusiasm was typical Hollywood, my fragile ego did inflate to the size of a tractor tire. Yes indeed, said the several voices now on the line, ABC back in New York, Fox Hills, everybody had *flipped* over the Monroes.

I was now soaring up over the Wind Rivers. "But what about revisions?" I said from the heights. Surely there had to be a comma or two I could change.

"Well," came back the voice, "there is a small, rather general change. Then there are some details."

Oh-oh.

"First," the producer continued, "because of programming policy on the network level, ABC wants you to . . . I'll give you their exact words, Otis, so you'll have the concept of it: 'Color it bolder.' "

I held the phone away from my ear and looked at the cowboys. They weren't exactly listening; they were shuffling their feet, but neither were they leaving.

"What did you say?"

" 'Color it bolder,' " he repeated. "More action."

"Well, goddammit, there's action in every story. There's a hook at every ending."

"Yes, of course, and they're beautiful, buddy. Nobody is questioning that. Please don't think we're questioning anything. But the ABC program people, they love the animals and all that incredible survival stuff . . . but they do want more action, jeopardy. You know. I mean, somebody comes in the saloon, or there to the Monroe cabin, and gets into a fist fight with Clayt. Or there's a shoot-out in the town, with the miners."

"Where the hell are the miners?" I cried. "I didn't write any miners in. There weren't mines here."

"Well, anybody then. Rustlers, guys who are going to lynch Indian Jim, maybe. Incidentally, that would be great right now, with all the race interest, civil rights ideas. The point is, we've got to have plenty of action to hold the kids."

My face was hot. "Look, what I tried to write was the truth about the frontier. Now you're putting it right back in some sound stage, the usual crap of saloon fights and shoot-outs. It wasn't like that. People were too tired. They had too many other problems in just staying alive . . ."

"Otis, listen. We *know* what you've caught here. It's priceless. But the big change is, ABC is so much in love with it that they don't want to program it like *Peyton Place* any more."

"What?"

"This is highly confidential. It's not out yet, I wouldn't mention it to anybody . . ."

"For God's sake, who'd I mention it to up here, and who'd care? Now what about ABC changing it?"

"An hour, Otis! They want us on as a full-hour weekly in color. How do you like that?"

"Well, I wish to hell I'd known before I wrote twenty-six *half-hour* stories."

"We'll still use them. Blow them up into hours, that's all. And you see, the gimmick with the hour is, you've got four commercial breaks in there. So each show has to be structured so you've got some action . . . gunplay or a fist fight every fifteen minutes. That will hold the audience over the commercial. It'll work, I tell you it will. Your stuff will stretch beautifully . . ."

I sat down, leaden. The cowboys frowned faintly at each

other, like I'd just heard of somebody being killed; then they began to drift outside into the sun where their horses were tied.

"Now, Otis," the voice continued, "I've put this all into a memo to you but I'll give you the gist of it, so you can start right back to work. As fast as you write—it'll just take you a few hours. Got a pencil there . . . ?"

"I don't know. Maybe I can find one . . ."

Fifty minutes later they had it all outlined, change by change, color by bolder. And in a rosy glow of back-pats and Otis buddies, said goodbye. I slumped in the ranch-house chair and whispered, "Those sonsofbitches."

They know not what they do. Hmmmm?

Well, they did know. And, frankly, when the long memorandum of changes arrived from 20th Century Fox, it was not as bad as I feared. It merely reflected the main threat to creativity in television: too many people. Writing by committee.

Perhaps you've had this experience. You watch some television dramatic show, and when it's over, you turn blankly to your wife and say, "What happened?" In other words, it didn't play off. You got to the end and a half-dozen red herrings were still around, the mystery wasn't really solved. It appeared that at the last minute something vital like the heart had been cut out.

It undoubtedly was. I've worked on shows where even writing and/or producing the damn thing, when I came to the end I was as confused as the audience. The cause for a show getting Greeked up can be many things: production changes, running over budget, or a story that wasn't right to begin with and in revisions simply fell apart. Then the studio, network, ad agency and somebody's mother-in-law all panicked into changing this, inverting the sequence of that until you have a Chinese puzzle that even the film editors can't save. As Jack Webb used to say, "It's like pulling one piece of yarn out of a sweater. Pretty soon you unravel the whole damn thing."

Well, we had a lot of yarn pullers: the independent production company, Mother Fox, the studio and a variety of nameless writers from programming *and* sales, back at ABC. The first major change dealt with the title of the series. It was originally *Them Monroes*. Now, this title and indeed the concept had been created by a delightful and clever comedy writer named Milt Rosen. Milt was quite a student of the frontier, and apparently had uncovered a true incident someplace back in the 1880's: a family of orphans who took a fling at homesteading in Oregon. Starting with this premise, Milt ("Uncle Miltie," as he'd write me) created the Monroe family, did an eleven-page outline that had lots of warmth and some funny dialect. But when this was submitted to Fox and ABC, they felt it was too much like a situation comedy set in the West. They wanted the real McCoy, and at this stage, must have felt I could deliver it.

I'd heard rumblings of this background in our initial meetings, and Milt was very philosophical (though burned up, I'm sure, and I don't blame him). Anyway, he communicated to me some fondly held and valuable thoughts about the show, albeit with a warning: "Needless to say, I don't agree one whit with any of the comments from the network. But when do we ever?"

Regarding the title, I'd felt from the beginning that *Them Monroes* with its double m's was too hard to pronounce. "Drop the them m," the boys said. Then you had *The Monroes,* who could just as well be a family of ice-skaters in Panorama City. I missed a ring of the West in the title: think of *Bonanza, Rawhide.* As I studied the Monroes, I saw them as orphans in a cow country, and you called an orphan calf a "dogie." "Git along, little dogies." People had heard that word, and the ones that hadn't, it would grow on. So I'd titled my novelette *The Dogies.*

"ABC did not feel," read the memo, "although we certainly did, that the '*doggie*' title was strong enough or all-encompassing enough for the project."

"Who," I cried, "said dog*g*ie? It's dogie. Dough-gie!"

The title had been spun into the novelette like a fine thread. Rip it out. Then make Clayt more of a hero, more decisive. (My protest: how can an eighteen-year-old farm kid from Illinois know how to do everything right in this wilderness the first time he tries it?) And don't let the Wales' boy . . . he's a loutish nester kid, sort of an animal . . . don't let him look lasciviously at our pretty Kathy Monroe . . . not at seven-thirty at night, buddy. Okay. And in that threatened Indian attack on the settlement (the Monroes and a few homesteaders are holed up in their cabin, wondering if the war party will come their way) "the network would appreciate your not alluding to the possibility that women and children might get killed. As we discussed, let's make the possible victims old men [senior citizens!]."

Waaaa . . . ?

Anyway, fellas, didja read the story? Nobody gets killed; the Indians never do attack. It's just the threat of it, hanging over, the suspense. Don't you see . . . ? Waiting is a kind of jeopardy, too. It was like that on the frontier . . .

Okay, okay, only senior citizens will be threatened to be killed.

And, finally, the Indian, Dirty Jim, stumbles on the Monroe family in the middle of a lightning storm. He's hungry, wet, tired. As he flees, reaches the top of a rise, he's struck by lightning. A bolt flashes down the barrel of his rifle. It hurts him bad, stuns him. An Indian here in Sublette County was knocked off his horse exactly like that, and wasn't right in the head for weeks thereafter. So Jim is suffering temporary amnesia, you might say, which is the only plausible reason our tenderfeet Monroes could possibly capture a wild Indian and then nurse him back to health. It becomes the bond between Jim and the family. Did you read in the novelette, there was about a half-page describing the terror of lightning in this mountain country . . . ?

Yeah, read it, but want it beefed up. "You see, ABC is a little concerned with the amnesia problem. Perhaps we should compromise here, Otis, and have Jim in a semi-state of amnesia."

Semi-state of amnesia? Fine, fellas. You're paying the bills. You can put him in a Nehru jacket if you want.

In defense of the writing committee and the sales boys, they did make some good suggestions too. They seemed particularly taken by a one-armed cowboy character I'd created, name of Sleeve. He was a mystery man, with the quiet dignity of the frontier in him. Perhaps he'd been a Confederate officer or killed someone someplace. He was a gent and a strong authority figure. They wanted me to write him into more shows, maybe have him work up a little "thing" with Kathy Monroe. Not quite, fellas, he's twice her age. Then let Clayt hero-worship him. All right. Thereafter, the memo confined itself mainly to shuffling the sequence of some of the stories. These ideas, I felt, were constructive. Instead of taking Clayt away on an Indian war for a three-parter, we'd cut back to the log cabin with an intervening story of Kathy, the Twins and Amy. Sort of a "meanwhile, back at the ranch."

So I rewrote the novelette the way they wanted it, bold colors now. It did occur to me, about halfway through, that if we were going to do an hour show once a week, then none of these stories would fit. Half-hour construction is as different from an hour as a Lincoln Continental and a cow pony. But they said it would work, so tap away, bundle it off, and I did.

What came back in a week or ten days was not another phone call but some of the producers themselves in the flesh. We squeezed them into our little hutch and had a good time. They were awfully nice fellows, persuasive, talented, excited. There was only one trouble. For the three days they stayed with us, the skies opened up and dumped. First hail, then a monsoon that old-timers say comes about once in every five Augusts and probably straight from Japan.

So I got the pickup truck, put it in four-wheel drive and we sloshed and slipped around in greasy gumbo mud. I'd take the producers into a potential homestead valley. "Now, up there," I'd say, "is a beautiful timbered ridge, beaver ponds, pine. You could set the Monroe cabin in the basin . . ."

"I can't see any basin. It's all rain and fog."

"Maybe we ought to hike up there?"

Well, we didn't hike any place, and the clouds got so bad they'd mist the truck windshield and make your clothes stick to your back. My back, anyway. At length, when the fellows couldn't shoot any location pictures and we'd rambled around enough, they reached the conclusion that to shoot *The Monroes* right on my ranch would be pretty much of an engineering job. First we'd have to lay in miles of road for all the trucks, then find bed and board for probably a hundred people. None of our hostelries close at hand could put up more than twenty; Pinedale being a fifty-two-mile round trip meant door-to-door travel time for all these golden-houred crafts and guilds. So it wasn't really practical to shoot on the ranch, and I breathed a sigh of relief.

On the day the producers were leaving, we sat down over a cocktail. I'd told them that because of my book commitment, I only had time to write the series novelette. But the trouble was, they said, if they hired somebody else to do the pilot, he'd have new ideas, changes, screw it up. Certainly I wouldn't want that, not after what I'd captured? The Monroes had now become part of me, and I was the one who should do the script. When they mentioned the price tag they had in mind, the ranch finances looked rosier and even the Beverly Hills remodeling might be paid for. All right, fellas. I caved in, went to my typewriter and whacked out a pilot synopsis. We shook hands and the producers drove over to Jackson, eighty miles. The next day they called from there. This was the place: hotels, lodges, fabulous scenery. A production man was being flown up from Fox to find locations. All he needed now was a script. I'd already found a title: *The Intruders.*

At first I thought it would be an easy job, but I wasn't half done by the time we returned to California in September. Then the real shock came. We drove up the driveway at Benedict Canyon, and there stood a resplendent, lovely remodeled house. Who built this place? I thought. Me? Good God! Teddy ran inside like a little girl, danced over the mellowed bricks of the new stone foyer, splashed in the glossy bathrooms. And here was a superb, mammoth closet where she could lock up all her treasures when we went off to the ranch. And the kitchen: counter tops, built-in appliances. Even my office, hardwood floors, recessed file cabinets: no more working in that arthritic little room over the garage.

Well, we clucked and walked around it: new landscaping, minimum of upkeep, automatic sprinkler system, fireproof slate roof. A home and a castle.

Home? But where was home? Didn't we just leave it at the ranch?

I never had a chance to answer, because the phone rang. Fox must have tracked my route by helicopter, for I surely hadn't told them when I'd arrive. "How are you doing, buddy? Everybody's waiting for the pages. Production meeting tomorrow morning. We'd like you in on the casting too. Have you got enough of a scene written so we can use it as a screen test?"

The next few weeks were insanity. We had gang meetings at the studio; the ABC program people were jumping in with both feet. As the pilot script evolved, I was told to squash the first six half-hours of the novelette down into a total playing time of fifteen minutes. This now resembled a trailer for coming attractions: cut, zap, bing-boom, there's your story. But it was still too long, ABC said: cut it to twelve minutes. Aw come on, fellas, it can't be done. Yes it can. "We drown the Monroe parents in a minute-forty; bury them in fifty-seven seconds . . . no, that's too goddamn long. Indian Jim is in, snap, lightning, that's about thirty-five seconds until he's flat on his ass, with Monroes mothering him. Dissolve, roll the wagons, cut of a moose here, elk there: wilderness, survival, eight seconds, and here they come thundering down the hill. The valley! They cry. This is *our valley* where poor dead old Paw was going to homestead. Give that a minute and a half, wrap it up . . . you're twelve minutes into picture and ready for the story to start."

Beautiful.

Why my typewriter didn't rise up and belt me across the mouth, I don't know. But somehow it got done. October became a month they'd forgotten to put on the calendar that year. Fox was sending messengers over to the house to pull the pages out of my machine as I finished them. These were mimeographed in about sixty copies for the production men; then there were last-minute changes because so-and-so had just been added to the cast and he didn't talk like these lines: scrap that dialogue and write new. "See ya in Jackson, buddy, on location!"

Neither Teddy nor I was very enthusiastic about going, but I suspected if I wanted to preserve what was left of my script, I'd better go up and baby-sit. We caught a jet, and once we'd settled down in a Jackson hotel, I invited some of my rancher friends over to see how TV westerns are made.

One cowman named Sam came all the way from Montana. He has the real West deep in him, runs a good ranch and is a well-known rodeo champion. Sam observed the first day's filming, leathery-silent. When we came back to the hotel he had a stiff slug of whiskey and muttered, "Otis, I have never seen so many guys pissing money down the drain as I saw here today. Standing around, drinking coffee, moving trucks, setting up them reflecting boards, jiggling lights: take that again, send the horses back the way they come. Why, goddamn, if I ran a ranch as sloppy as this, with so many deadheads, I'd be belly-up in a year."

We went back the second day. Now, in one of the opening sequences of *The Intruders*, the action stuff, the script called for a fight. Poor Indian Jim, the beanbag, caught it from the tough cowboys. Jim's horse was dumped on a sandbar in the river, the cowboys roped him and ran him down. "That's much too violent," I protested. "It wasn't written that way."

"They'll love it," the production people answered. "We'll take full responsibility."

Sam was fascinated by the stuntman who made the horse fall for Indian Jim. "Now that feller," he said, "knows his business. But these actors, Otis. Hell, most of 'em you're going to have to hogtie on a horse if you intend 'em to ride in these pictures."

"We have already tied one on," I told him. Not really tied, just gave him a nice thick rope under the saddle blanket he could cling to in times of emergency.

It was a brave new world for my friend Sam. He'd ask me quite often about the salaries. "How much does he make, say that dumb sonofabitch standing over there holding that hammer?" I'd tell him the union carpenter wage per hour and he'd shake his head. Then he'd begin studying the cast like they'd just stepped off a slide under a microscope. He'd noticed the actors and actresses making their way to a massive, sleek trailer that was hauled through streams and into pine forests, everywhere we went. "What the hell is that thing?"

"They call it the Honey Wagon," I said.

"What's it do?"

"It has dressing rooms and individual toilets for the cast."

Sam blew out a long breath and sat down on a log. "Je-sus Christ. Individual toilets."

"You can't get 'em to go out on location without it. Union rules."

Sam left then and went back to his cows. But now, after a few days of filming, the townspeople of Jackson had discovered a new pot of gold. It seemed as if all the local girls had fled to the beauty parlors, and what emerged was a steady stream of flossy teenagers, bowling-ball hairdos, eye shade—anything to attract a look from the movie producers. Out on the location, one young cowboy ambled up to me. "Say, mister," he said, "how do you go about gettin' discovered?"

"Hang around, I guess."

"Hell, that's what I been doing. I even got a job wrangling this stock of yours. But the only time one of them producers looks at me, he hollers, 'Hey, kid, bring that horse over here!' I guess I ain't cut out to be no actor after all."

Miraculously, the weather held: golden autumn days. The cameraman was overjoyed. He was getting pale azures, purples, vermilions that you can only really see up here in the altitude and the clear air; and the camera accentuates them. But even the wonder of film can't take care of everything, as we were to learn.

We'd come finally to the epic "discovery sequence." After twelve minutes of zipping and zapping through the wilderness, the Monroes finally came over a crest and saw Father Monroe's homestead valley. (This was not going to be the real valley they'd live in during the series, because the production people hadn't found that exact valley yet. I said, "Wait a minute. The audience is going to know." The boys smiled and said, "Don't worry about it. We'll make a few cuts here and there and the audience will figure the real valley for the series is just behind the camera. Hell, it's all pine trees and hills, all looks the same anyway.")

Rushed up from Beverly Hills, now came a monstrous truck and camera boom that would lift so high the director and cameramen looked like butterflies on top of it. Who knows, maybe they were. Everything was set, the wagon creaking to the crest of the hill, Clayt on his splay-footed farm horse, Indian Jim on his paint pony; Kathy driving, baby Amy beside her, the pots and pans jangling on the wagon and the Twins running in the yellow grass behind.

"Roll it."

Down came the wagon, thundering, clattering, Clayt yipping and Jim hollering Hollywood Sioux war cries.

"Cut." The camera boom lowered so the director could come back down to earth. He talked to the cast. Something went wrong that time. Maybe Kathy didn't spout enough tears of joy, for the camera on the boom was moving close to her face. Send the wagon back up the hill, do it again.

Oops. That time, somebody fell off his horse.

Again.

It took most of the day, but at the end, the crew was overjoyed. We really caught the feeling of these poor kids traveling fifteen hundred miles, lost in the wilderness, and finally stumbling onto a monument of rocks their father had built: the valley, their new home.

It was not until weeks later when the footage went into the cutting room that some astounded film editor said: "Hey, fellas.

You've got these beautiful shots of coming into the valley. You've got these beautiful reactions, close-ups on Clayt, Kathy, Jim looking out at their valley for the first time. Where is it?"

"Hah?"

"Where is the goddamn valley? A picture of the valley?"

"You don't have one?"

"Not a frame of it. They might as well be looking at Sunset and Vine, for all we got."

Panic, phone calls, recriminations. There was three feet of snow now in Jackson and we had no picture of the valley. Match in something from the California mountains? Wrong kind of terrain, wouldn't fit. Finally some bright-eyed kid strolled in from the publicity department. He'd happened to snap a color still of what the Monroes were looking at. He'd figured that if this was the Monroe valley, we'd certainly have it on film and we'd want a still of it. Hallelujah! The still was run off into enough feet to look like it had been filmed, and through the wizardry of cutters and editors, the Monroes did get their valley after all.

But Teddy and I were long gone by now. We'd driven over to the ranch and stayed about a week. We'd never been there just the two of us, without kids and guests. Nor had we been up for any length of time in the glorious fall.

Out in the ponds and sloughs along the river, I shot a few ducks. We'd dammed up a big slough, and the first year, working like a rice farmer up to my knees in water, I'd planted duck feed here. The payoff was great flocks of birds, including some species such as canvasback and pintail that don't belong in this country. They had no fear. They'd swoop and dart over me. Once, walking on a bluff beside the river, I surprised about a hundred Canada geese sitting on the bank below. I was so astounded it seemed like three months before my shotgun came up. I hit one and he dropped in the river, then swung to another, but they were gone now, out of range. Sheba, my Lab, was already splashing into the current to pick up the bird. But that goose, seeing the flock thunder away, gave a massive beat of his wings, leaped off the water and followed them. I watched him for a long time. He never dropped. Sheba had swum across the river and was running aimlessly back and forth in the willows. She couldn't believe it either. As I stood there in the autumn afternoon, I had a strange thought for a hunter. I was glad that bird had gone free.

Then the time came to sell our calves. This meant a lot of riding and sorting for several days. Finally the big diesel trucks rumbled in; the mother cows bawled and mourned in the corral as the calves were taken away. And the buyer sat on the fender of the truck, dirty-fingered, and scribbled me a check. We'd contracted the calves to him in July, on a handshake. It was as direct and different from Hollywood as the gnarled roughness of his hand. I wondered why all of life couldn't be so straightforward and trusting.

On our last day Teddy and I took the *Big O,* my tin boat, hauled it by truck several miles up to the north end of the ranch. Here we put it in the river, complete with a lunch, wine, Teddy's pillows and her knitting. She's not a fisherwoman. I traumatized that out of her when I took her fishing for a month and a half on our wedding trip. So she lay in the bottom of the boat and we drifted on the crystal water, ducks and geese skittering off, moose around the bends, slogging up, staring at us.

Teddy was reading my finally completed first draft of the medical book. She's a good editor and she's honest. I can cuss hell out of her but she won't change her opinion. I usually tighten up like a turtle in his shell when she reads my work. But somehow today it didn't seem to matter. Even fishing was lousy—water too cold, the trout had migrated. They knew winter was close at hand. I flicked away, as fishermen do, stared at the multicolored pebbles passing under me. Finally we hit the big pool where Gladys, the moose, had run me out. I was casting lazily with a yellow woolly worm on, not paying attention. A suck of water, tight line. Out in a spray of sun leaped a rainbow, his side stripe flashing crimson. He darted and fought, hit the heavy eddies, bowed my rod. "I want this one," I breathed to Teddy.

"Play him slow."

"Don't worry. Dammit," I cried, "I forgot my net."

There we were, a superb fish sounding, running, leaping. Teddy scrambled past me and dumped out the anchor. Now the boat held and I got the fish downstream, began to drown him. It must have taken fifteen minutes before I nursed him alongside the boat. This was the critical time. I could see the fly, worn loose in his hard lip. I slid my hand into the water, caught him behind the gills; he slapped me nobly but I had him, flipped him into the boat. When I held him up, I couldn't believe the beauty: orange,

94

silver, gray, red—a wild fish. Not big, four pounds. I've taken larger ones, but none somehow with the significance of this lone rainbow who was waiting in the river that day.

I had the courage then to ask Teddy how she liked the book. I watched the tilt of her chin and her eyes for any telltale wavering.

"It's an awfully good start," she said.

A start? I thought. Hell, it's a finish. I'm through with it, aren't I?

"It reads very fast. You've covered so much, and made it dramatic. But I do think it's going to take more work, more medical details. You'll have to interview quite a few other people to support these different scientific findings. You can do that when we get back to California."

"Drudgery," I muttered. "But I suppose it's got to be done, once the Monroes are out of my hair."

Then I looked at the rainbow in the bottom of the boat. The sage smell, the distant pines and eternal quiet seemed to sweep over me. "I wish," I said, "we didn't have to go back down there. Just stay here, the two of us like this. Never have to go back. Do you feel like that sometimes?"

"So much."

"Why do we go back, then?"

"Because you have to be there, darling," Teddy said. "You want to do TV, can't afford to cut yourself off from it. Besides, Beverly Hills is still home in a way, at least for the kids. Their friends are there. And frankly, we enjoy it too. You come into contact with people, get book ideas . . ."

"Now you're giving me my excuses back. You don't really believe that?"

Teddy stared at the river. "I don't know what I believe. We've been round and round on it so much I'm frankly tired of trying to figure out where we do belong."

Here we are again, I thought. The same old decision. Do you give up a kind of security, break completely with what you know? And the odds on the Wyoming end weren't that convincing: to be sure, the land was a fine investment if you could afford to hold it, but the cattle business was a rough trip even for the old-timers who knew what they were doing. The ranch would always be marginal, and the writing of books more so. I could see some awfully bleak winters ahead, between inspirations. When you sit down with the lonely page of a novel in a typewriter, you don't know if anybody is ever going to see it or care. But in Hollywood, there was always a new series beginning, somebody with an idea to develop. The market was alive; you were in the swim and available for hire. And yet, I thought, to try to live in both worlds seemed to be an increasing clash of cultures, a constant tearing and a feeling of never finding yourself. I didn't know how long I could keep doing it. In fact, it made me wonder whom we were living for: careers, friends, ego, family? Live for everything but ourselves.

I looked at Teddy then, the sun on the side of her face as she trailed her fingers in the water. "Aw hell," I said, "I guess we just can't figure it out now. Maybe we never will."

That was as close to the truth as I knew right then. I plucked the oars a few times until the boat was at the landing, and we went home.

# 8

A funny thing happened on the way to the medical interview. I was walking down Bedford Drive in Beverly Hills, lovely day in November. I'd gone to buy a note pad and I was hurrying out for an appointment with an educator who knew a lot about brain-injured children. Subject of the book; fill in the technical details, as Teddy had suggested.

Suddenly, Bedford Drive and the chic shops and pretty people began to spin in front of my eyes. The pavement under my feet became spongy, as though I were walking up and down little concrete hills. What in the hell? I thought. What's happening! Then my hands went cold. I was weak. I loosened my tie. There was a gas station on the corner, about fifty yards ahead of me. I knew I had to get that far. And I was terrified. My breath was very short now, my head floating like a balloon.

I woozed my way to the gas station, found a dime and plugged it into the Coke machine. Needed blood sugar, I'd now decided. I was probably tensed up, run out of energy. I sucked a little of the Coke and fumbled it into the rack. Then I got to my car, which was nearby, and drove home.

When I came into the house, I found Teddy mothering her china and arranging it in her new cupboards. I told her what had happened. She was puzzled, suggested I phone the doctor; I really should have a checkup. It certainly wasn't anything serious, though. Then she called the people I'd been going to interview and said she'd come instead, take the notes.

Well, I lounged around for a few hours, feeling sheepish. By that night, we were joking about it. My father, we recalled, had been troubled by dizzy spells for years. His was an inner-ear condition, leading to deafness. Maybe, we diagnosed, that's what I was getting. Sure. That was it. Or it could be my eyes. You reach your forties and they begin to wear out. We were pushing more amateurish probing pins into my body than a voodoo effigy. Every place but in the head, which apparently was too hard. And then we forgot about it.

A couple of days later I was back at work revising the medical book; I was typing, slogging away. I usually whisper the words aloud as I write. But suddenly there was an audible ping, like a pressure valve letting loose; I felt my left eardrum pop. Then dizziness swept over me. I got up and ran from the typewriter. Whatever the symptom was, it seemed to indicate flight somewhere. I went to the kitchen, gulped milk and cookies. That afternoon my doctor tapped and measured me for a while. He concluded it probably was a blood-sugar condition, nothing to be alarmed about. Suggested I have a midmorning snack, take in some protein, and, "Quit pressing yourself. Stop working so hard."

Re-lax, buddy. Just like that. Shut it off.

We tried to. Thereafter, about midmorning, Teddy would come padding into my office with cold cuts and milk; I felt like an Indian nibbling pemmican or jerky. But still, when I'd go down to the studio, or drive some freeway to an interview on the book, the old sways and swims would begin again. "Let go, let go," Teddy had said. And I'd wonder how I was going to get through the meeting.

At night we'd try to figure it out. "Obviously," Teddy'd say, "something is bugging you. What is it? The house here, being more or less rooted down in Beverly Hills?"

"I love the house. Who wouldn't? Play tennis after lunch, take a swim. We've got everything here, good friends, diversions. Even the work in the studio is so wild that it's exciting. I know I need the stimulation of this place."

"But you want the books too. And the tranquillity of the ranch."

"Yes, I do. I'm neither fish nor fowl. That's a lot of the trouble."

Teddy nodded. "Wanting your cake and eating it. You always have. The performance-oriented society says you can't let go of the big image of success. But you'll have to one day, to find your real self, your authenticity. I wish you'd read . . ."

"I know," I said. Beside her chair, she had several books, some spiritual and others by philosophers and psychologists. One of these was an outstanding thinker, Adrian van Kaam. A Hollander who'd served in the Dutch underground during World War II, van Kaam was a priest, psychologist and head of the Institute of Man at Duquesne University. We'd gotten to know him at a married couples' retreat, and his concept of spirituality in the modern world was deeply moving to me. But like the drunk who hasn't found the bottom of the bottle, I wasn't ready yet; or perhaps I was too busy or afraid to look into myself. It was just easier to postpone any day of reckoning.

By now, finally, *The Monroes* pilot was completed; I found much to argue with in it, but the superb scenery and perhaps the bumbling in making it did seem to charge the film with excitement, a sense of reality. It hit Madison Avenue sometime around Christmas, and by early January, five or six advertisers had bought participations. The series was alive and living in Hollywood—splashy publicity, blue-sky thinking and counting the money. Then ABC proclaimed our time spot: eight o'clock, Wednesday nights.

It sounded like a beautiful position for the show: prime time, middle of the week, family viewing. But a closer look revealed some thorns. Our lead-in audience, which is vitally important to the success of any show, would come from none other than Robin in Gotham City: we were scheduled to follow *Batman.* Now, everybody knew *Batman* had been a smash for a year or so; but when you live around the TV mills long enough, you begin to anticipate the squishy fickleness of audiences. If *Batman* began disenchanting the audience in droves, that meant they'd be switching to the other networks. And what was the competition there? On CBS, *Lost in Space* (another Fox show, by the way), and on NBC the hefty, well-produced *Virginian.* To make matters worse, both of these programs began at seven-thirty, which meant that their audiences were a half hour into space or the *Virginian*'s Wyoming before *The Monroes* even came on. Were we to assume that the audience would just switch from these popular shows and come join our little family in the cabin?

The fellas at the studio said, Re-lax, we'll wipe out the competition. Then they added that they didn't have a producer yet. Why didn't I take it? The production people who had put *The Monroes* together would be busy with other details and launching more shows back at the studio. Hell, I'd be up lazing around my ranch all summer, just two hours from the location. Why didn't I move Teddy and the kids over to Jackson, hang in during the weeks of production and go back and play cowboy on the weekends? Money in it, buddy.

At that point I couldn't have produced a roadside lemonade

stand, and moreover, didn't want to. I knew *The Monroes* series was in for a rough trip; it would have to overcome a bad time spot and also the creative committees that had already picked apart its flesh. But nobody seemed worried, and finally I just tried to put the future out of my mind.

The problem was, you can't endlessly devour your own intuitions. They have a habit of sticking in your throat. At the same time I was trying to swallow my long-forgotten novel, *The Paper Bullet*. It had taken nearly a year and a half to worm its way through the publishing mills. I hoped there was a motion picture in the book. By now, you see, we were nicely bogged down in Vietnam, just as the French woman had predicted. People, I thought, are going to want to know how we got there. They'll get the message out of the book.

The movie studios did a read on it, said, Yeah, it was a good dramatic yarn. What else is new? Well, I thought, when it picks up some strong reviews, maybe gets reprinted someplace and starts to sell, the producers will take notice.

As the reviews began to trickle in, I couldn't believe how bad they were. Only a few reviewers seemed to get the message. The book didn't crash. It dropped silent as a pin on a pillow; a state secret gets more publicity. Teddy and the publishers were sympathetic; it just went to show, they said, you can't put a message in books. Get off the soapbox and tell a good story. And by then, the publishers had read my draft of the medical book. They were pleased. This was safe stuff—oh, controversy in it, sure, but about kids and learning processes of the brain. Every mother had a kid, didn't she? They'd eat it up. While I was having lunch with the editors in a little New York restaurant, this swallow choked me too. I got the dizzies and sweating hands; finally I broke off the lunch, excused myself and Teddy and walked for miles up Fifth Avenue.

Soon thereafter the publishers gave me a massive memorandum of changes. The first draft moved well and was a fine start, they said, but now I really had to put in all that medical background they knew I wasn't able to research properly up in Wyoming. (Who was worried about the brain up *there*?) So I should start laying out a sequence of interviews; there were men I must see in Alabama, New Haven, Indiana, San Francisco. About three months of travel and interviews should wrap it up, then rewrite the draft with the medical specifics in place. Hire a medical consultant and another from education.

Hold it, boys. "This is a hard admission to make," I said, "and I should have done it long ago, but I'm not your man. I'm in over my head. I've lost interest in the project. I can't take it any further."

"But we truly want you to."

"I appreciate that. But I'm out of it. I don't feel right to do it. I'm going to refund you enough of the advance royalty so we can hire a properly trained co-author, a good scientific writer. He can have my draft and go from there . . ."

It was a big wrench to walk away from three hundred and some pages of manuscript, better than eighteen months of work. But I didn't do it selflessly; it was sheer necessity. I couldn't write two lines for Mickey Mouse now; the whole act was pain. Everything I'd worked for, the values I'd had, seemed to have collapsed: there was nothing left to fill the vacuum.

I prayed then for a meaning in my life. For a humility that would help me accept myself and the world I'd made.

But you don't turn off the faucet quite so quickly.

The spells got worse. I didn't want to go to the studio, face a typewriter. I didn't want to do anything but maybe lie on a beach in the sun, hear the roar of the sea.

About then Teddy made a wonderful suggestion. "Let's go to Hawaii," she said. And we did, on a slow boat.

I wriggled in the black volcanic sand of Maui for a couple of weeks, and it helped. Teddy and I surfed, took long walks; she learned the hula and we seemed to dance our way back through time. I hadn't returned to the islands since the war, but I'd missed them. They represented the freedom of youth, when you could fall in love with a *pikaki lei* and the girl in it, have raucous parties on dark beaches, drinking Japanese sake we'd liberated on Guam. Now, out here again, the faces of old friends came back to me as if the firelight was still on them.

I remembered too how it felt, out beyond the reef, when there were four of us in a silver plane, flying the last flight eastward, going home. In the old days in the Solomons, we'd fly for a thousand miles and never see an American ship. But that July of 1945, in the entire distance from Okinawa to Pearl Harbor, there was

101

beneath us a steel chain of battleships, destroyers, carriers, transports; not once were we out of sight of a U.S. ship. It was an emotional experience to look down on such power. The crusade was over, the world saved, we thought. Go home, you lucky ones, and live the life you want. You. Your dream now.

The day we were to leave Maui, Teddy and I drove leisurely through the green hills and terraced plantations that splashed down to the sea. We didn't care if we caught the Pan Am plane that night or the next or whenever. We stopped at a beach and lolled in the surf. When we boarded the jet at Honolulu, I upgraded our tickets to first class. Teddy is too frugal to travel this way, so we never do; but this was a never trip. In the roaring takeoff, with a cocktail in my hand, I didn't look back at the islands. They'd served their time for me; you can't run to the past, only ahead. Perhaps the darkness that closed over us seemed to say that. In 1943 it had taken us sixteen hours to make that flight in a DC-3. Now, in a DC-8, four and a half. New world.

When we got home that night, Tom and Pete were still up, expecting us. "Boys," I said, "come into my office. We want to talk to you."

"Oh-oh," Pete said.

"No, it's not a lecture, really."

They sat down. I lit a pipe, looked around at my new hardwood floors, the built-in filing cabinets of the most luxurious office I'd ever have. "Your mother and I have decided," I said, "that we're going to sell this house and move to the ranch. I think you know that I've been pretty churned up lately. Maybe I always will be, but I honestly feel I've got to make this move. I will not do it, however, if you boys don't want to. If you feel it's too much of a jump for you. And I'm going to write this to John at school and get his vote too."

Pete shrugged. "I'll be going off to prep school anyway. Sure it's nice here, but who needs Beverly Hills?"

Tom, however, frowned, and scratched at his big mop of hair. "Gee, Dad, we've just remodeled the house. It doesn't make much sense to turn around and sell it."

"I know."

"It's an awful good house."

"Tom, you'll be going off to college a year from this fall. You won't be using it as much as you do now."

102

He pondered that. "Well, I know you've been worried, Dad. I mean, both of these places cost money; you've got the ranch to run. If it *is* money, though, I'll tell you what I'd rather do. I'll work for nothing on the ranch. So will John and Pete, and we'll get our friends to. Then we can afford to keep the house here."

It made me smile. We paid them precious little on the ranch. "I know you'd work for nothing, Tom. But it's not money. It's really just the dislocation of our life. You can't live in both worlds. I can't anyway."

Tom nodded. "Okay," he said, "that's that. Let's dump it, get out. It'll be kind of an adventure."

"We'll go, why not?" Pete said and slouched off to bed.

"I've really got to hand it to you kids," I began. I wanted to tell them how much I admired them. But maybe they knew.

"I almost dread calling Leila again," Teddy said. "Those real estate people and our friends are going to think we're absolutely nuts. We must be, aren't we?"

"Yep." I grinned. "Either that or we're beginning to see things clearly for the first time."

"Tell me that again?" I said on the phone. "They're going to do *what* to the Green River?"

"Make it a Wild River," my friend answered. He was calling from Wyoming, where he was involved in politics and water matters.

"What the hell does a Wild River mean?"

"Some headaches for you and other ranchers. In fact, it might even put you out of business."

"Aw come on. How?"

"Because they want to condemn a strip of land a quarter of a mile wide on each side of the river, turn it over to the public."

"They can't do that! On all these ranches, the houses are in that strip. So are the ranch buildings, corrals, ditches . . ."

"Like I told you," he said, "it's serious. You'd better think about coming up here. This is going to be quite a fight."

A few days later I got a telegram from one of the Wyoming senators, asking me to appear as a witness at a Senate hearing on the Wild River proposal, to be held in the high school at Green River City. Then, in the mail, I received a preliminary Interior Department study on the Wild River, complete with maps. My heart sank. The strip of land to be condemned did indeed snake right through our ranch, following the river. It would cut the heart and guts out of the place. There was even a provision for a paved road running along the river near our house and slicing the ranch in two. If this wasn't enough, they'd add a site for an amusement park (on a Wild River?) just north of our heifer pasture.

Here we were, trying to sell the place in Beverly Hills and move to the ranch, and now Wyoming appeared to be going up in smoke. Exhaust, that is, and fishermen and hunters' cars, picnickers, shooters, looters. I knew one thing: even if they moved our buildings outside the public zone, it wouldn't be safe to stick your head outdoors. You might as well try homesteading in the Battle of the Bulge.

Neither Teddy nor I knew what to do. We'd had no experience with conservation and even less with Wyoming politics. But the reflex of a writer is to find out facts and then fight back with words. I got on the phone and called my neighbors. To these hardy ranchers in Wyoming, any intrusion by the government is suspect at best, and the reaction was practically unanimous. A majority of people in Sublette County were bitterly opposed to making the Green a Wild River. So was the governor, and the Wyoming delegation in Congress, with the exception of Senator Gale McGee. That seemed good enough for me. But then, one rancher friend disagreed. "I ain't sure at all," he muttered, "whether we'd better not get in and take this Wild River. Fix up the wording so we can live with it. Because if we don't, I just got an idea that the state is going to turn around and dam us out."

"A dam?" I said.

"You bet. For forty years they've been talking about putting in this Kendall Dam, a few miles below your place. It would wipe you out and the whole valley with you."

"So it's kind of either-or, but they get you both ways?"

"That's about what it comes to."

I wish now that I'd listened to this man. For what he predicted came true. Only a handful of us realized it then, and the greater tragedy was that our stretch of river and valley became a hot potato tossed back and forth between the federal government and the state of Wyoming.

Actually, both sides, federal and state, had a plausible case. They just went at it wrong. In the Study Report on the Wild River, which is a noble idea, the Interior Department should have realized that each proposed Wild River had a different problem in terms of ownership of bank lands. For instance, some rivers in Idaho flow almost totally through already-public lands, federal- or state-owned. There are a few pieces of private ground along the banks—mining claims, homesteads. Since these are usually abandoned, they can be condemned by the government with little hardship to the owners. To classify such a river as Wild means that you keep roads, dams, development, timbering, mining or motels out of it. I couldn't agree more.

But here on the Green, it was obvious that the old-timers had settled big ranches, grubbed hay meadows and made large investments in sweat and money, directly alongside the serpentine river. To ask these ranchers to give up their bank lands to the public was tantamount to asking a private homeowner to yield, say, his four-foot entrance walk through his front yard, through his house and out the back. Give it over to the public, and then

105

have the effrontery to tell the homeowner that he can still live and operate his business in his home.

Such a scheme was patently impossible, and every rancher up and down the Green knew it. Moreover, they also knew that the public already had full access to float the river, fish it; the only prohibition was going up on the banks, on private land. Wyoming, with its landowner-dominated legislature, is very strict about trespass laws. As strict, say, as a factory owner would be if he didn't want the public wandering through his plant all day long.

But there was a solution, which I could see even then. Though it might take patient selling to some of these leathery, independent ranchers, I felt it could be done. A Wild River on the Green would prevent any dams, any future junky developments or polluting industries that would destroy one of the last real wildernesses in the United States. Now, the rancher didn't want any of these things either. So my idea was: use the concept of the Wild River, not as a condemnation of bank lands, but as a zoning. The ranchers would agree to a zoning that would guarantee in perpetuity that their ranches would remain as they are at present, untouched by dams, roads, industry, etc. To be sure, I knew that the ranchers, with their natural suspicion of anything "government," would consider such zoning as an infringement. They worried about "Washington changing its mind, grabbing our land someplace down the road." But the risk seemed to me worth taking, for in the long run it might be the only way to preserve our lands for those who wanted to enjoy a truly wild river.

I wrote this recommendation into my testimony before the senators at the Green River High School. But I was already too late. War had been declared: Wyoming versus Washington. Tempers heated up; nobody listened to anyone else. No one tried to rewrite the legislation, at least not in time to save the Green. Later, ironically, in the less passionate halls of Congress, the Wild Rivers Act was amended to include what were called Scenic Rivers. In these, there was no condemnation of private bank lands. Instead, it was tantamount to a zoning, protecting the river as is, which was what many people had hoped for on the Green.

But, in the political pressure, we fell between two horses, and the Green was omitted from the bill. It wasn't too many months

106

before the state of Wyoming would begin to plan exactly what my rancher friend had warned: build the Kendall Dam, wipe us out.

There's a story they tell around Cora about an old-timer who used to take eastern dudes hunting. John, the old fellow, couldn't read or write. Once, just before hunting season, a dude sent him a telegram. John knew it must have something to do with a planned trip, but just what, he couldn't figure out. So he took the telegram to a rancher friend and said, "Harry, what do you make of this?"

Harry was wise to him. He glanced at the telegram and grinned. "Why, John, I think it's just fine, don't you?"

John grumped around a little, then said, "Goddammit, Harry, read it to me."

Harry appeared surprised. "Oh, I thought you knew how."

"Yas, yas," John said. "I learned in school, readin' and writin' both, only we never did get to tellygrams."

I wished I hadn't either.

When I came back to Beverly Hills and into the rarefied air of *The Monroes,* a couple of unctuous messages were waiting for me. They were from the ABC boys back in New York:

> . . . YOUR WONDERFUL PILOT SCRIPT WILL BRING US ALL GREAT SUCCESS AND SHOULD BE THE TALK OF THE TOWNS BOTH HOLLY-WOOD AND NEW YORK . . .
>
> . . . I KNOW IT'S BEEN LONG AND TEDIOUS FOR YOU IN HAVING TO CONTEND WITH NITWORK [SIC] FINKS LIKE ME. I ONLY HOPE THAT IN SPITE OF IT ALL THAT YOU ENJOYED THE RELATIONSHIP AS MUCH AS I DID AND THAT YOU WILL TREAT ME KINDLY WHEN YOU WRITE YOUR VERSION OF "ONLY YOU, DICK DARING" . . .

When I got back to the studio, a producer and a story editor had been hired, and writers were already breaking down my novelette into scripts. I could hardly wait to see the results. The producers told me they were going slowly at first, picking the best writers they could find in the hope that two or three would really "catch the magic" of *The Monroes.*

All the cast was in place. We were going to build our town I'd called Paradox on a superb site overlooking the Snake River. I felt confident that this was going to be a businesslike job; we had no place to go but up.

Crash!

The first, unkindest cut came when the Writers Guild of America decided on a strike sometime in the late spring. I forget the specific grievance, but as Guild members, it meant that all our possible writers, including myself, wouldn't be allowed to work. The strike would cripple every show and particularly ours, because we were planning to shoot on location in Jackson. The films had been budgeted by Fox to cost approximately $150,000 each. Location filming is always more expensive, and we'd need to have the majority of our scripts written and budgeted before we even went to Jackson. In this way, if we had a cowboy versus rustlers chase in Script 3, and a similar one in Script 10, we could shoot them both at the same time and save money. Budget is a stern taskmaster in television, and on the pilot, I saw some examples of how to go broke quick.

For instance, I'd written into the pilot an innocuous campfire scene: our little family sitting around the wagon, cooking a rabbit stew. In an earlier version of the script, Clayt had shot the rabbit on camera, but that had been cut out for time in our trailer, so all that remained was my mention of rabbit. But that was enough for some office functionary down at Fox. He air-expressed from Hollywood to Wyoming three live rabbits to put into the stew! Now I ask you. The Monroes weren't *eating* the stew. Just a movie, play-tasting. We could have put Wyoming mud in it for all the audience would know.

Also in the pilot, there'd been an unfortunate blooper in getting the Monroe parents to drown properly in the icy Snake River. Stuntmen of course were used, shivering in their rubber suits. But apparently one of the stuntmen failed to read the script or the water was too cold. Anyway, he didn't duck his head under and disappear like a drowning father should. So there we had a beautiful scene of the Monroe kiddies mourning on the bank while Father floats downstream a few yards away, so close that Tiny Tim could have plunged in and saved him. It made Clayt look like an unconscionable coward. How do you fix it? Well, you get in the special-effects people at X dollars an hour, and painstakingly they paint Father's head out of all the hundreds of frames of film.

108

Costs money, that's the point, and when you're long-range, on location, the price of each booboo is staggering. This was why, simply, we knew we had to have all the scripts in and pretty well deloused before we went to Jackson.

The proposed writers' strike changed that. The Monroe office became bedlam—phones ringing, writers being summoned from the Malibu beaches, the canyons and out from under rocks. Some we got were clearly part-time milkmen, gas pumpers or right-handed first basemen. Nice fellas—but the Real West, anyone? They'd never heard of it. The panic scripts were pure Sunset Boulevard.

I was appalled when I read the first ones. The Fox messengers were coming almost hourly to my house and dumping off bundles of scripts. Novelette? The twenty-six stories that ABC had bought? That was ancient history, that quaint survival stuff and how the pioneers lived in Wyoming. We had Hollywood cowboys now, straight out of the sound stages, saloon fights, plot number 6 multiplied by plot 4, divided by the old cliché number 13.

The writers had apparently fallen in love with miners, despite my dictum that there were no miners in Monroe country, and gold wasn't the story anyway. Then they introduced two tribes of Indians, Utes and Pawnees, who'd never set foot up here. I'd given the writers five authentic tribes who were in the country at the time, but who the hell cared? Next, they'd added a dog, a big-footed, floppy Alsatian who first entered the Monroe wilderness with a *cruel* master. The dog was going to be shot for killing sheep until the Monroe Twins save him. He becomes part of the family. In another show, a second *cruel* master steals him, puts him to work in a harness. Baby Amy saves him this time, or does she? I'd kind of lost interest. (Just to show you how far I'd drifted from the tastes of the American TV audience, the dog was a smash and they loved him back in Cedar Rapids and the Bronx. We had by then drifted so far from the original concept that I guess the poor sonofabitch was all we had left.)

But still the stories kept heaping in. There was another about a wolverine. In this epic, an Indian war chief died of a heart attack, moaning pleas to the "Carcajou" (Hollywood Indian for wolverine) not to wipe out his tribe. Later, grown homesteaders sobbed and a grizzled trapper went mad in fear of the wolverine. At this point in the story, I called Wyoming and talked to several of my friends, old-timers who ought to know. One echoed: "All that on account of a goddamn little wolverine? Hell, I been in the country seventy years, most of it trapping, and I never even seen one."

"What would you do if you had?"

"Spit in his eye, I reckon, and go about my business. Wolverine hide ain't worth nothing, not worth killing."

"Fellas," I pointed out, back at the studio, "this is really going too far. Now, if it were a grizzly bear, yes, people would be frightened of him. But nobody would get heart attacks or weep. They'd just go out and shoot him, and then get on with the real job of staying alive."

"Really, though," the producers answered, "we have to use the wolverine. ABC has bought some nice stock footage and they want it in."

So we got the heart attack, wolverine and sobs. When the monster finally appeared on the screen, he was about three feet long and the audience saw him for, at most, five seconds.

By now I could see clearly the direction the show was taking. Even the pilot film which had sold it was being recut, to add a teaser hook on the end. They'd promised me they wouldn't do that, but ABC and the group-think boys had changed their minds. Now remember, we'd already put the audience through a peril-a-minute trailer of drownings, lightning, roping, dragging Indian Jim, Clayt fighting, wagons set on fire. After this exhausting fifty minutes, the network demanded still more jeopardy. The editors were told to cut in a sequence of one of the Twins lost in the woods. Twin steps in a hole beside some fallen timber. His foot gets stuck. Then, off camera, a satanical scream. Cut to a mountain lion, padding in, licking his chops. What will happen to poor Twin? Tune in next week, folks, and see if some writer can figure how to get him out of it.

As the scripts kept flooding in, I got a drowning feeling. For a time I stayed in the studio offices and helped a valiant story editor rewrite the ones we thought we might save. And how were things doing on the home front? Well, our Benedict Canyon "Movie Star View Estate," resplendent in its remodeling, had now been photographed in a brochure that circulated to the vari-

110

ous real estate agencies. The bait was out: where were the fish?

Like most house sellers, we were convinced our estate was so superb that people would be standing in line to snatch it from us. Hardly. But, as spring drew on, and Teddy's garden flowered, we began getting a trickle of lookers. In California there are apparently many of these; ladies who have tired of bridge or couldn't get the girls that afternoon, so they drive out in the hills and peer into people's closets. I doubt if the average looker could have afforded to buy the abandoned gas heater at the swimming pool, but up they came, apparently preferring to travel with a real estate agent than to buy a map of "Old Movie Star Homes." Each time Teddy would clean the house and some flossy manicurist would troop through. "Gee, it's a showplace, honey. Gorgeous. Thanks for letting us look. See ya."

Slowly, though, qualified buyers did manage to find us. They were Stars. First, they'd send an emissary, usually their indentured real estate agent. Once this person had duly reported what we had, then a business manager and/or lawyer would arrive and we'd go through the same tour for these exalteds. Last, Star would appear. Frank Sinatra's team made several visits, then Dinah Shore's minions sent for her. We felt very hot right then. But alas, when you get those business types poking around, you can usually find a few leaks. With Dinah Shore, it was a matter of closets. She had several hundred dresses that demanded adequate hanging room. There was debate as to whether we could turn our master suite into one massive closet, but then where would Miss Shore sleep? The house stood on top of a hill; if you added another master suite you'd be someplace down the bank in the poison oak. With the Sinatra entourage, the problem was: where did we put the private heliport? We suggested the tennis court as a possible pad. But in the studio business offices, someone detected resistance to helicopters on Benedict Canyon, which already suffered a daily road traffic of about 13,000 cars. So Frank drifted away, following Dinah, and we were back to just plain folks. No, not quite. We still had one hope left, and for this lovely lady, I felt an urge to turn real estate agent myself. She was Elke Sommer, the German actress; she loved the house and invariably came to see it in skintight toreador pants and luscious blooming blouses. On our various trips around the grounds—I tried to make as many as I could—Elke told me she'd grown up in the country.

Bavaria, maybe? I'm not as acquainted as I should be over there. Anyway, she was titillated by our birds and flowers; once she spotted a dead mouse in the swimming pool, knelt down gleefully, dangled him by the tail and flung him away. Now, as I told Teddy, a girl like that really should have this house. Shades of Hedy Lamar.

But much as I wanted to jiggle the figures around, we never could come to terms. Elke was our most loyal supporter, and I still go to all her pictures.

By now our friends were asking, "Sold the house yet?"

"Nope."

"Good," they'd say. "Now you can forget this crazy ranch idea. Besides," as one friend of Teddy's pointed out, "you've got your ranch right here, seven beautiful acres in the hills. What else would you want?"

It was clear by now that our friends were worried—the gentle concern, say, that you show when somebody you love has been packed off to Menninger's. We were told repeatedly that our move to the ranch didn't make any sense. The primary objection seemed to be: "What will you do with yourselves up there? Who will you see? Who will you *talk* to?"

Myself, I thought, and that wasn't too far from the truth right then. By June, failing to hook any customer for the house, we rented it to a screenwriter and his wife, then took off for Wyoming. In the rental agreement, our agent was going to keep showing the house, and surely, we told ourselves, in a month or so, the phone would ring: sold, a bundle of cash.

Well, I didn't have much time to sit waiting by the party line. First, a couple from Beverly Hills, good friends, had asked to come up and hunt a bear. Since I'd never been on a bear hunt, I felt this was a fine time to start. Wrong again. Our friends arrived and, as can happen in Wyoming in late June, a storm descended, rain, then snow. The lady hunter, who's a distinguished actress, was really just along for the ride. This brave young thing is lovely, tiny, and arranging a vase of flowers is probably the sum total of her physical exertion. In fact, she had once broken her leg, her husband swore, getting up from a sofa. Anyway, she had a sleek new bear-hunting outfit and gamely insisted on going with us.

Now, bears have very inconvenient habits, around which the

technique of hunting is built. First, you must go far up into the timber, and here, taking into account the wind and availability of cover, kill some large animal: an old cow or, in our case, a dying workhorse. Then you allow a few days for the carcass to begin to rot; the bear smells this, and with his predilection for foul meat, he starts dining on your bait. But he ventures forth only at, say, five in the morning or nine in the evening. Therefore, at these atrocious times, you have to be hunkered down in your blind, moving nary an eyelash. In certain cases, the bear approaches the bait from behind, and if you're quiet and beautifully camouflaged, then he'll lumber directly through your blind, really too close to shoot, but you might be able to pet him if you wanted.

This, in short, was the chase our dainty actress friend had signed on for. The first night and next morning, we clunked over sagebrush hills in the pickup truck, then walked three miles more in driving rain mixed with snow. When we got into the blind, we were shivering so hard that our cut branches and mottled tarpaulins palpitated with creaks and patterings any self-respecting bear would have fled from. Our hands were trembling so much we couldn't light a cigarette, the rain leaking down our necks until finally Dave Shannon accomplished a miracle. The entire forest was soaked by days of rain, but Dave skinned sagebrush back until he got down to the core of dry wood, then shaved this into tiny slivers. He blew and nursed until we had a roaring fire, plus apples and candy bars that a friend, Dick Thomson, had produced like the loaves and fishes. No bear tonight, but at least we were alive.

Our Beverly Hills friends stuck it out bravely through a couple of more such stands. Then all of us decided that bears really weren't that stupid. Probably they didn't like rain or cold any more than we did, and so they'd curled up in some nice warm den to let the storm blow out.

When it finally did, we drifted up to the blind on a beautiful morning; it was about noon, banker's hours. We thought we'd picnic and doze a little. We talked, laughed, smoked, and finally did take a nap. Then somebody whispered, "Look!" In the warm sun, a lovely brown bear was munching away on the carcass. My hunter friend fired a couple of times and that was the end of the game. We later discovered that the bear had been napping herself a few yards from the carcass: damn sensible animal, we concluded, and a lovely trophy.

What we had not figured on, however, was getting the bear home. After we'd cleaned her, the hunter, Dick and Teddy went back up to the timber in the late afternoon. Because of some emergency on *The Monroes,* I wasn't able to go with them. They got the bear slung over a pole, then had to carry the dead weight of her down a canyon and up to the truck. During this time Teddy pitched in to help, strained the bear over the creek and then felt a knifelike pain in her back. When she came home that night she couldn't straighten up. Often, in later months, she'd go into lower-back spasms, finally sought out a revered osteopath in Beverly Hills. "Now, Mrs. Carney," he asked, "just how did you get this injury?" He was probably thinking of the usual California whiplash in an auto wreck, or at least something acceptable like putting American twist on a tennis serve.

"I got it," Teddy said proudly, "carrying a bear."

The osteopath has now retired from practice.

Because Teddy is so active, loves to ride and work outside, the back injury was an added annoyance to her. But she'd managed to cure her ulcers, and in the same dogged way she resolved to lick the back. She began doing a series of grim exercises every morning; I tried them for a week and dislocated my neck. But she kept at them and finally beat the bear and the disk both.

"You know," I said to her, "our story is beginning to sound like *The Perils of Pauline.* I wonder what's next?"

I didn't have to wait long to find out. A few days later I was down at the Cora store buying fishing flies. I'd picked up our mail because we only had once-a-week delivery. There were some Monroe scripts and the usual junk stuff; then as I lounged around with the cowboys and had a beer, I noticed an envelope from the Principal's Office, Loyola High School, Los Angeles. It would be some mimeographed summary of the school year, or a touch for a new building campaign.

Oh-oh.

A typed letter. About Tom. It began slowly. Tom had not done well at Loyola: attitude bad, wrong friends, seemed to be a center of troublemaking. Then it picked up pace, and in the final paragraph the headmaster concluded that Tom was not their kind of boy. They were reluctant to take him back.

When I returned to the ranch, I found Tom and his brothers fixing fence. I asked him to come into the homestead cabin I was now using as my office. "Damn it, Dad," Tom insisted, "I didn't do all the things they put in that letter. Sure, I haven't had a very good year, but they're tagging me with stuff I'm just not responsible for."

"It comes down to this, Tom. Do you want to stay at Loyola or not?"

His eyes filled up. "Well, sure. I don't know where else I'd go, after blowing Hotchkiss and now this."

"Then you'd better sit down and write the headmaster the finest letter you've ever written. You're going to have to earn your chance to stay in school. It's just that simple."

Well, Tom did send off a very earnest letter. And I added one of my own, making the suggestion that he be put on probation until he proved himself in grades, conduct and general attitude. I felt confident he could do it if they'd give him one more chance. A week dragged by. Finally a letter came from the headmaster. He'd gamble with us. Amen.

By now the summer was rushing by. There never seemed to be time to do what you wanted: glorious clear days, the runoff over, the river splashing with fish. Again I had a feeling of wanting to retreat from the outside world: get a book started, perhaps, or if not that, to root into my log cabin office every morning, read and think. I was groping for an answer, not only for my own disorientation and the physical symptoms of the dizzy spells, but for the anomie and growing disenchantment of the American people. It seemed as if we were being cut adrift, youth morose and rebellious, and more adults all the time breaking with the traditions that had raised them. So was I, and I found it a distinctly uncomfortable process.

But I didn't get an answer or a book. Instead I was swamped with more Monroe scripts. My job was to authenticize them; I rewrote quite a bit of dialogue, talked by phone to the producers in Jackson, and finally felt I'd better go over and see what was happening.

I made several trips to the location that summer. Watching a movie being made is painstakingly dull, slow, but there is a sense of camaraderie around the cast and crew. You watch endless takes of a man reining in his horse and delivering a short

115

line. First the horse doesn't stop on the marks, so the actor's head is cut off by the camera; then a distant jet lays a rumble in the mike; then the actor blows the line. Quite soon you've drifted totally out of reality. You don't know where you are, and in my case it was even more dreamlike. For here I was sitting on the main street of Paradox, the tent city I'd created. And the characters I'd given birth to were strolling around me, smoking cigarettes or squatting under a wagon; bubbling, as most actors do, with irrepressible enthusiasm: what a terrific series we were making. The audience really ought to eat it up. Then they'd say how lucky I was to live on a real ranch in this superb country. A fellow'd be crazy to want to go back to Hollywood, right?

Right.

But one of the actors, a roping champion and authentic cowboy whom we'd cast as Sleeve, put it a little differently. "Otis," he told me, "I'd rather ride a thousand miles than say one line of this goddamn dialogue. Can't you do something?"

"I've tried to, Ben, but we don't get very far."

"It's too heavy with talk, and what action there is looks phonier than hell. All they'd have to do is turn the camera loose on these mountains, this scenery. Public would go for it, I know."

I knew it too, and so did many others in the cast. But the message never seemed to get through to the top. By now the scripts had been finalized into bulkily plotted, multi-charactered clichés. There never seemed to be time left over to build our family or to do the warm quiet sequences that give reality. It was go-go-go, long talky scenes connected by cutbacks to various sub-plots, and eternally, every fifteen minutes, somebody pulls a gun or fights with his fists.

Soon I stopped visiting the location. The script corrections I'd made had almost invariably not been used. There were good excuses: my comments arrived too late, or such and such scene had to be shot as is because a prior scene, tying into it, had already been filmed. In a few cases the producers came out and said, "We think you're really being too authentic. After all, people don't care about little details, not when the whole show has so much quality and richness."

But keep working, they added, keep adding your ideas. It was, as they'd promised at the beginning, a very pleasant relationship. We were just talking different languages. And perhaps the producers realized this too, because soon I noticed that the scripts were coming to me *after* they'd been filmed. It was really easier that way: story consultants can be a helluva bore when you've got a schedule to meet.

So I went home then, back to the ranch, and tried to forget the Monroes. "It's going to be a disaster," I predicted to Teddy.

She smiled. "Not totally."

"What do you mean?"

Then she glanced at our son John. "He's been working on something."

John lounged over, grinning, and unrolled a long sheet of paper. "I guess this may surprise you, Dad. It's a plan for the house."

"What house?"

"Ours," Teddy beamed. "And John did every bit of it!"

I was astounded. John had not quite turned seventeen then, but for years before, he'd decide out of the blue to take a day off from school. He'd get his pencils and light board and design office buildings, houses, shopping centers. He was fascinated, too, by machinery, and saved all the baler and tractor brochures that came to the ranch. The antiquated haying process bothered him, so he'd spend hours designing new tractors, assembly-line methods of making and picking up bales. And yet, for all John's engineering aptitude, he was the one who could master guitar, piano, write his own songs, paint pictures, and then, in his relaxed, uncompetitive way, go out and win a track meet for his school.

As I studied his plans, I could see the plot he and Teddy had hatched. This was the big house we'd always hoped to build on the oxbow above the river. But now? I shuddered. *The Monroes* was in trouble, the Green River situation a mess; we'd either have a dam or a Wild River. We could get condemned out and lose a lot of money. Further back, down in Beverly Hills, we still had a house that wasn't selling.

"But really," Teddy said, "what you're afraid of is permanence, isn't it? Eventually, you know we're going to sell the house in California, only you're not sure you want to move here . . ."

"I've just told you the reasons why it's impractical."

"But it's not, darling. Please listen. We've been worried so long about where we're going to be that we never quite get settled any place. Well, I've thought about that too. We're only going to have the boys a few more years. Once they're gone—it'll happen before we know it—the only thing we'll have left is the memories of the times we had here, in a proper home for all of us."

"Besides," John added, "Mom says you'll be getting some pretty good royalties out of *The Monroes*. I've cut this house down so it will be simple to build. I know we can afford it, Dad."

I was outgunned. Maybe, indeed, I'd been thinking about it for a long time but didn't want to face it. Because this was the final leap. With a house of our own, we'd settle at the ranch someday soon. And I knew I wasn't ready yet, not with the Monroe dream turning into a nightmare; no book to write, and little confidence in myself ever to begin one again.

But still, some voice in me said that I must gamble this last time. We called a carpenter in town, Harry Lovatt. He was from a pioneer family in Pinedale, an ex-Seabee and one of the finest gents I've ever known. Harry had built the little house for us, and now when we showed him John's plan, he said, "We'll do it for you, Bill and I."

Bill was an ex-coal miner and a wonderful carpenter. He and Harry worked as a team, just the two of them from the ground up. There was no contract except a handshake. "We get $3.65 an hour," Harry said, "and I'll put ten percent on it for materials. Show you where we're at every month so you can call her off if you're worried."

"I'm not, Harry." With men like him, you wouldn't be, ever.

An architect friend back in Chicago refined John's plan in certain details. "I'm amazed," he said, "that a sixteen-year-old kid could draw up a house like this. If John ever wants a job, he's got one with me."

Then Teddy and I drove to Salt Lake. During our time in Utah, we'd fallen in love with the old-fashioned Mormon houses which were built of a sand-colored stone called pot rock. We tracked the pot rock to a quarry. In the pioneer days there'd been enough labor to cut it into large blocks. Today this would cost a fortune. But once we saw the rock in its gnarled, natural state, lichen growing on much of it, we knew we had something quite unusual if we used it in rough pieces. In addition, as the wise old Mormons realized, it was superb insulation against heat and cold.

A week or so later the quarry owner arrived with twenty tons of pot rock on a massive truck. We didn't dare take him across our creaky ranch bridge, so we unloaded by hand and lugged over every piece ourselves. It was dusk when we finished, and we were exhausted. As I stared at that mountain of rock, looming on the bluff above the river, I knew I was committed.

I saw the premiere of *The Monroes* twice. The first time was in a motel room in Rock Springs, Wyoming. We didn't have a TV set at the ranch, let alone color, so we went to the Outlaw Inn for the night. Dave and Mike Shannon and a couple of their friends were with us. We downed enough bourbon to steady our nerves and then switched on ABC. The transmittal of color in western Wyoming is still an exotic art. Though I recognized the Tetons from the shape of them, the show was brilliantly smeary, as if you'd melted down a box of crayons. As I watched, my face turned red as Indian Jim's; I felt hot, dry-mouthed. A certain scene would come along, like Father Monroe drowning in the Snake River, and I'd wince, remembering the painted-out frames. Then, in another scene at the cattle-baron's camp, production had become so lugubrious that a snowstorm intervened. The camp was covered with powdery snow that the audience never saw fall. In playing time, the scene was only supposed to take several minutes. How do you explain an instant blizzard? Again, call for the special-effects men, paint in some snow, make a dissolve and then write a line to the effect: "You never knew what was going to happen in Wyoming." So I winced there too, and wondered how the public would accept such a cheat. Then came Twin in the last jeopardy teaser, foot stuck and the mountain lion roaring . . . hoo, boy! But to my surprise, not only Teddy but our Wyoming friends seemed to enjoy the show. Sure, they admitted, there were some obviously raw spots but the Monroe kids were pleasant and the scenery lovely. I felt encouraged. Maybe I'd been too hard on the show; the audience was apparently so starved for something different, they might put up with us after all.

A few nights later I attended the big bashy premiere at the 20th Century Fox studio theater. Everybody had turned out for it, from the humblest horse wrangler to the loftiest front-office executive. I took the liberty of bringing Tom and his impresario friend, Richard Correll, producer of "The Legend of Hairy West." On the big screen here, the color was superb. When the film ended, the audience cheered, pumped hands and embraced. Buddy, we had a winner! On the way out of the theater, I found

Tom and Richard. "How'd you like it, boys?"

"Gee, Dad," Tom said, "I'm amazed. I'm sorry, but that's not the show you wrote. They've loused up the whole idea."

"Mr. Carney," Richard said, "it stinks. Our picture was better, no kidding."

"A helluva lot better," Tom added.

Before I could get a full review from the adolescent section, Really Important People and their wives began surrounding me, purring their praises. It was a warm glow that carried through highballs and finally back up to the canyon home. Teddy, by then, had heard the boys' reaction. "Oh"—she smiled—"you know how kids are."

"That's what bothers me. I know they're damn perceptive. You can't put anything over on them. Just look at *Mad* magazine. These kids can sniff out the phoniness of the adult world and harpoon it by reflex."

But a writer's frail ego often jams up his listening apparatus. You believe what you want to hear, and we heard plenty when the returns came in. On the *Good Friday* book, I thought I'd received a lot of mail; in comparison, the reaction was an avalanche. I was overwhelmed and grateful for the letters, but my God, I thought, the power of TV! Didn't anybody do anything but sit in front of that idiot box? People I hadn't heard from in years, and who never knew I'd written books, were now writing me from distant outposts. They loved *The Monroes*. Bully. Bravo. They'd clip out reviews from the hometown papers. Can this be? I wondered.

Chicago *Sun Times:* ". . . Shows excellent promise of becoming a triumph . . ."

Chicago *Daily News:* ". . . smacks of realism and authenticity . . ."

Chicago *Tribune:* "We hope *The Monroes* stays with the story line established in the opening episode . . . that of a wholesome family . . . and doesn't degenerate into just another TV western . . ."

And finally, from Olympus, Jack Gould of the New York *Times:* "The premiere was so reassuring there is really no need to check on the well-being of *The Monroes* for the rest of the year . . ."

Amplify reviews like these in the echo chambers of Hollywood, and the Fox people began dancing in their studio streets. I still couldn't believe it. When you're too close to a film, or a book for that matter, you can't possibly judge it. But you do have an instinct, and mine tended to agree with Tom and Richard Correll. After all, these kids had grown up watching TV. They knew!

Then came the first bomb. I was over at the studio when the New York weekly *Variety* arrived. The reviews here always tend to be stern and uncannily perceptive. The production people didn't seem to be bothered at all, but I read every word as if I'd written it myself.

"The video road west," said the *Variety* review, "has been working its way further from the old style morality play actioner toward psychological melodrama and now reaches what could be its apogee in *The Monroes,* a full-blown soaper-oater. While it is several cuts above the daytime detergent serials, *Monroes* shares with the daytime shows the lump-in-the-throat approach to life and the peril-a-minute approach to drama.

"Both approaches were handled well in the initialer, although sixty minutes of tragedy, near tragedy and rescues from tragedy may prove to be a bit much even for the more avid fans of highly charged drama. While this opener may have been purposely loaded with these high-tension incidents to grab the viewers early in the season, the producers appear to be banking on an unlimited public appetite for emotional violence and not a little physical violence . . ."

Color it bolder, anyone?

So the other shoe had dropped, the one I'd been dreading for months. But again nobody seemed to be listening. *The Monroes* was alive and running, chock-full of advertisers. The first rating came in and was flashed over intercoms. We had a good audience share—bound to build, wasn't it?

Then they saw the second show.

After a few days of respectful silence, there was a brief article in *Variety,* explaining that ABC and Fox had been insisting *The Monroes* would go on for years, become another Ponderosa Ranch and Cartwright family. Forget it, fellows. Have you seen the *next* shows? *Variety*'s headline said it all: "Yes, We Have No Bonanza."

In the strange way that life works, I have now, perched in my office, along with my shotguns and flyrods, a Charley Russell bronze. Cowboy on a horse, with a plaque below:

Western Heritage Award
of the
National Cowboy Hall of Fame
and
Western Heritage Center
presented to
The Intruders
(The Monroes Series)
Outstanding Western Fictional Television Episode
of 1966
and to
Otis Carney
writer.

By the time I received my little horse and the winsome cowboy, the audience had seen perhaps a dozen of the next shows. And they knew and we knew what I'd feared for so many months. *The Monroes,* despite the warmth of the kids and the scenery of Wyoming, had been botched beyond repair. Change concepts, try this, that, hire, fire. Talented men began frantically trying every medication, but the patient was too far gone. It was, I knew now, just a matter of time before the Monroes rode off to the last roundup.

But Hollywood is a tomorrow town, and people were coming to me, on the strength of *The Monroes* pilot, wanting to make deals. There was excitement about using my abandoned Sam Eagle character as a rugged nineteenth-century cowboy who rides his horse into neon-lit Las Vegas. I did a reluctant tight-fingered story treatment, earned a few thousand dollars and my own self-scorn for polluting a helpless character like Sam. Next I was hired to do a screenplay about Mexico: true story of a doctor who mined silver down there during the revolution. This idea had appealed to me, for the doctor's anguish was existential: did the doctor make himself rich, or did he abandon the chase and rededicate himself to his fellow men? It didn't matter, really. I got my money for the doctor and Sam Eagle; they went into some filing cabinet, replaced by new ideas and more promises.

Then on a March day, a voice on the phone said, "Otis buddy?"

"Yes . . ."

"Look, we just talked to New York. ABC is delighted you're going to do the last script of *The Monroes.*"

I am, I thought, like the obstetrician: helped bring the monster into the world and now I've got to knock it on the head.

"Of course," the producer glowed on the phone, "you realize this is only the last script of this current Monroe filming. We're pretty darn sure we're going to get our pickup for next year's series in just a matter of hours . . ."

"Yeah."

"Now come on, we're going to do it. They love us back on Madison Avenue. Another network wants to buy the show, that's also in the wind."

"Yeah."

"Now if you've got a few minutes . . . got a pencil there, I'll give you the comments ABC had on your outline. They think it's a really cute idea. But they do want a lion."

"What?"

"I know how you feel about mountain lions. But this is a tame lion, see, an African lion."

"An African lion in Wyoming in 1879?"

"I know it's tough, but you see, ABC has learned from their audience profiles that the lions on *Daktari* are really responsible for the success of that show. Of course, Judy the Chimp figures in there too. But this lion bit, the kids love 'em, as fast as you write it, won't take you any time to doctor the script, bring in the lion . . . hell, he could be traveling through . . . Buddy, you still there . . . ?"

Not really. I had put the phone down and was staring out the window at hummingbirds in the orange blossoms and the restful Benedict Canyon hills. Somewhere on the litter of my desk was a memorandum I'd written months before to the network and the heads of television at Fox. I itemized where I felt the show had gone off the track, and then outlined a new concept for *The Monroes,* in which Clayt starts to build a ranch, Kathy gets a job teaching school. I wanted them to have responsibility and *do something,* not just play around with chipmunks until some Bad Person fell upon them.

"Honest action," I concluded, "is still the basic appeal. In my opinion, this show cannot be a Disney-cum-Lassie approach. If it's meant to be, then we'd better redesign it and make Clayt a captor of wild game for zoos and museums. By all means use animals in their habitat, but not as a focus for the eight-year-old mentality. If we are to do 'Daktari West,' then let's own up to that fully and throw away the rest. My vote is no. I don't think it will work . . ."

But months later, after the memo had been clucked over and filed away, here came the African lion. The lion ventured into 1879 Wyoming with a traveling circus (I've yet to see my first mention of a circus in any of the pioneer accounts). Forget that technical stuff! We got a lion and a midget and a strong man, plus miners who die in a cave-in. The cave-in undermined the town of Paradox, by now a veritable honeycomb of abandoned shafts after all our mine shows. Goodbye, town. Clayt and his little family are moving on anyway, don't need you any more. And here's a great idea for a title: *The Ghosts of Paradox.*

There was no bronze memorial horse and Russell cowboy this time. Only the faint puff of the silencer as the ghosts and the African lion and my typewriter administered the *coup de grâce.* What about the pickup from the network for the new series that would come in a matter of hours? The phone never rang. Approximately five million dollars later, a lot of fresh trails cut by the Honey Wagon and a thousand blank cartridges, *The Monroes* was dead. "Dead for good" as my boys used to say, when they played cowboy in Utah.

In Beverly Hills, I'd watch the cars streaming down Benedict Canyon. Thirteen thousand every morning, people hurrying to work. I'd look close at the faces. Here was a magnificent California day, no smog yet, the canyon damp in the haze of sprinklers, soft green hills, banks of ivy, coveys of quail dusting along the road.

But nobody saw them. Not those faces in the cars. The drivers were clenching their steering wheels, setting their jaws, racing to pass some slower car before the next bend. They were not thinking of now, this one blessed moment of their life. They were thinking two, three hours hence, down in the office: what they'd say to so-and-so, how this meeting would go, what the market did, what the trade papers said. Thinking ahead, planning, controlling. Thus, these people couldn't feel a tingling in their wrists, a pulse in their heart. They couldn't see the majesty of the world they raced through. Indeed, they didn't even enjoy the breathing of a rich suck of air.

I was no better than they. I was equally caught up in the performance world, the chase. This was the vibration of city life, the so-called stimulation that rasped your muscles and nerves until you couldn't feel anything but the iron bowstrings of your own tautness. You said to yourself, society told you that you dare not fail: that's why you hurried, planned ahead, even in your roaring death-missile automobile, sweeping down the canyon . . . you planned how to get yours, succeed!

And if you did fail, what? Admit it? Realize that the whole game had no meaning anyway? But no, you couldn't admit that, any more than you'd stop your car on Benedict Canyon, stretch in the lovely sun and smell a flower.

Because you couldn't admit you'd failed, and were cut off from feeling . . . it had been trained out of you . . . you dared not mourn. Big boys don't cry. Corporation men must keep going up, up, up, rising curve of earnings yearly.

Once, about the time of *The Monroes'* demise, I'd been asked to meet the producers for luncheon. The place was an exclusive Hollywood restaurant; you had to be a member. The big people in the networks, studios and agencies came here in tribal ritual. Being a guest, I was shown to the table of my hosts. Things were awfully busy at the studio, so I expected them to be late, which they were by a half hour. I sat alone at the table, had a tomato juice which I felt was a bolster against a potential dizzy spell. From where I sat, I could see the dark Tudor doorway, watch the VIP's enter. Some of them wore straw hats, which they'd skim to the hatcheck girl or give her a wink and a squeeze. Almost all of them carried leather dispatch cases, which they planted at their feet like loyal dogs when they drank and dined. You could never afford to be very far from your Madison Avenue–Sunset–Vine lunch pail; you might have an important memo in it, a selling point, a story outline which, after a bath of martinis, you'd bring out and sell during lunch.

As I watched the various Bigs entering, a strange thought struck me. Their expensive suits and business charm seemed to melt away. Suddenly they were like little boys, in those magical years between eight and twelve. And they were play-acting: dress-up. They'd put on Daddy's clothes, and here they were in grave earnestness, manipulating numbers and symbols, drinking grown-up cocktails and lazing pensive and hard-boiled over forbidden cigarettes. Little boys, their whole lives dedicated to impressing the other fellows, using play money to buy corners of a sandbox or a fistful of marbles. And the dreadful part of their game, these little boys believed it. They thought they controlled the world.

Watching them did indeed make me mourn: for them, for me too in the years I'd spent like them. I swallowed hard and my eyes stung, remembering: the advertising agency in Chicago, Cinerama, all the big-shot roles I, too, had played.

Now somehow they were done. The rewards didn't seem to matter any more.

It was April then, Los Angeles already balmy in the spring. People were down at the beaches, kids out playing ball. Tom was playing at Loyola. Our remodeled house and garden never looked lovelier. In the last days before we left for Wyoming, Teddy showed our new tenants around. Failing to sell the house, because the real estate market was awful, we'd signed a seven-month lease with a young show-business couple, actor Ryan O'Neal and his actress wife, Leigh Taylor-Young. They'd worked together on the Fox show *Peyton Place*.

Then, on April 17, Teddy and I made our usual walk down the long driveway to the mailbox. This was to be a big day for Tom, his eighteenth birthday and the time when he'd hear from the various colleges to which he'd applied. His first choice had been Princeton, perhaps because I'd pushed him toward it in the typical proud-father way. However, earlier in the spring, an Admissions representative from Yale had showed up at Loyola. Tom was recommended to him, and in an interview the Admissions man seemed intrigued by the Western movies Tom and Richard Correll had made. He suggested Tom come back and show them at Yale, which Tom did.

When Teddy and I took our mail out of the box, the top letter was from the Admissions director at Princeton, addressed to me. It had been a hard decision, the director wrote, but they didn't feel Tom was qualified for Princeton; they feared that with his history of ulcers, he wouldn't be able to stand the pressure. I was sunk, didn't even glance at the rest of the letters. But Teddy had. She held up a fat, official-looking envelope from New Haven. "Ote! He must be in Yale!"

When Tom came home that afternoon, he ripped open the letter and kept walking around the new brick front hall, shaking his head. "I can't believe it," he said. "I really wanted to go to Yale all the time, but I never thought I had a chance. The only chance I'd have would be at Princeton, because of you and all the family."

"Because of you, Tom," I said. "You did this on your own."

When I left for the ranch a few days later, I felt our life was finally straightening out. In the blossoms of spring, the long trip seemed familiar and very refreshing. I hurried, because I was driving alone. Actually, I had Buck and Sheba, the bird dogs, but Teddy had decided to fly to Salt Lake with Carmen, our Mexican cook.

The first night out of Los Angeles, I pulled into a little town in Utah. The skies were brooding, the cedars whipped by wind; it was raw cold, spitting sleet. As I drove toward Salt Lake the next morning, big wet snowflakes were falling. I couldn't believe it. I wasn't that far from California. It would take Teddy's jet only an hour and ten minutes to make the trip.

I hurried toward the Salt Lake airport, arriving about noon in a black, violent blizzard. I was late; her plane should have already landed, the weather so vile I dreaded for her to be flying in it. As I swept toward the entrance of the airport, I couldn't even see down the runway. But now an ambulance passed me with a wailing siren, then police cars. A policeman, his face wet with snow, waved me to a stop. "Turn around," he said. "No traffic into the airport."

"I'm meeting a plane."

"Can't go in there. Sorry. There's a crash on the field."

"But what plane, what line?" I cried.

He'd already gone behind me to the next car, ordering everyone to turn around. My hands were limp. I kept peering toward the field: all I could see were the hazy amber lights of fire engines. Then I snapped on the radio, drove toward Salt Lake. Prayed, too, until an announcer cut in on a program. It was a jet from Denver, another airline. Fortunately, no casualties. Tore off the landing gear, blocked the one-instrument runway. The reason: Salt Lake hadn't expected this violent spring storm any more than I. They'd put away their snow-cleaning equipment for the year, and because the runway was so slushy and icy, the jet couldn't stop.

From a motel room, I finally reached Teddy. Her flight had been grounded in Las Vegas. I told her to get on the train. This wasn't California any more. This storm was going to stay for a while.

The next morning I met her and Carmen at the station. We went up through the Wasatch in snow and fog. Big diesel trucks had jackknifed off the highway. You couldn't see ten feet on the interstate highway or in the mountain passes; but still there'd be a honking behind me, a car would swing out and lurch blindly by. I counted enough of them to realize almost all had California plates. Hurry, get there, make time count.

But the real significance of the trip didn't hit me until we drove up Cora Road. The snow was still banked along the fences, and there was a fresh three or four inches on the road with no tracks through it. A horse trailer had skidded off and the driver was jacking up, putting on chains. I couldn't see the Wind River mountains; even the pines looked chilled, their limbs dripping and soggy. And someplace down below, the major leagues were playing ball, friends were catching the surf at Malibu. "So this," I said to Teddy, "is where you want to be?"

She laughed. "You will, too, someday."

Even in that awful weather, our prospects did brighten when we saw the new rock house on the bluff above the Green. Harry and Bill came out to meet us, and they'd accomplished a miracle. Except for a few inside details, the house was finished. Out of rough cedar, Harry had made all the cabinets and woodwork; Teddy's stone floor in the living room was a triumph. Harry and Bill had worked in the house the entire winter, just the two of them. Mind you, the house was partly open then, the west wind whipping through it: slightly drafty, down at twenty below. But Harry and Bill would light a fire in the living room hearth, work with gloves on. Every day that winter they'd driven twenty-seven miles out from town, then off-loaded their supplies on a sled Harry had made. He towed this a mile across the river on his snow machine. I wondered how many builders you'd get in the city or suburbs to do such a house? And when the last nail had been hammered, Harry and I settled up on our contract, which had been sealed only on a handshake. He had missed his original eyeball estimate by no more than a couple of hundred dollars!

It was always a shock, when I'd come up from Beverly Hills, to meet again the honesty and ruggedness of these people. For instance, during that winter just past I'd heard how an old man at a cow camp above us had been feeding the elk for the state. Apparently he'd hung his harness on the side of the log hay crib, and one young bull elk hooked it with his horn. The elk was startled, and with the harness dangling over his horns, fled through the timber toward the mountains. The old man cussed at him, then put on snowshoes. For the rest of the day, until dusk, he snowshoed after that elk until, at the top of a mountain, he finally played him out. With the elk panting in the heavy snow-drifts, the old man leaned down and lifted his harness from the horns. As one cowboy observed, "Hell, why didn't he just shoot the sonofabitch there at the feedground and save all that tromp-ing?"

Why didn't these people behave differently, sensibly we'd say, in a lot of ways? This was a question that began to fascinate me. And perhaps I got my answer from another old-timer who lived a few miles north of us. His name was Gus Galinat; he was a homesteader who'd come here from Lithuania, settled a 160-acre tract of ground and built his own cabin and barn. Even since the early 1900's, Gus had lived on this hard-bitten patch of ground. I'd tried to get to know him over the years, but Gus was deaf, suspicious of newcomers. He'd hide in his cabin when we'd come by. He was a bachelor who lived alone, always had. His skin was as wrinkled and brown as a cornflake; he had wispy white hair. I'd be floating down the river some afternoon, glance at the thick willows on the bank, and I'd see a little piece of Gus. He'd be still as an Indian, watching me. He knew every fish on that river; he ate mostly whitefish, grouse and game meat. Rarely would he go to town.

Sometimes, after the first years, he'd ask me over to his cabin, which was a masterpiece of broad-ax hand-hewn architecture. Gus was a superb carpenter; around the turn of the century he'd emigrated to the United States and helped build the Park Hotel in Rock Springs. He worked in the sawmills up in the timber, and then for Abner Luman on his vast ranch. Gus never ran any cattle himself. Sometimes he'd lease his 160 acres to the neigh-bors, but he wasn't much of a businessman. He didn't really care. More often than not, neighboring cattle would rub down his buck fence and pasture on him. They'd walk the old ditch that never ran water. Gus and others had dug it with a horse and bucket scraper, God knows how many years before. But the survey had been faulty: you can't push water uphill.

So eventually Gus had returned to the woods. Now he'd grin at me in the dark of his cabin. "Yah, I got a crazy patch."

"A what, Gus?"

"Crazy patch. Here, I show you."

He'd take me out to his log-hewn shop, which was littered with his handmade skis and snowshoes. From the rafters he'd pull down burled pieces of aspen. I'd never seen gnarled limbs like these, nor did I find out where Gus's crazy patch was, because he wouldn't say. But out of these pieces of aspen, he made furniture, candlesticks, statuary of animals. He supplied several dude ranches around the area with aspen and pine chairs that are masterpieces.

In the fall, visiting with him in his shop, I noticed an ashtray on a pedestaled base which had a burl at the bottom and top. It was beautifully carved and even had a container for matches. As an inveterate pipe smoker, I wanted this piece if he'd sell it. You never knew with Gus.

"Yah," he said finally, "I sell him. Nine dollars. T'row in dem candlesticks too."

I tried to pay him separately for a curving pair of triple candlesticks, but he wouldn't do it. Nine dollars. All I had was a ten, so I gave him that. Several months later, in the winter back in Beverly Hills, a scrawled envelope arrived. Enclosed no letter, just a dollar bill, my change. Now, in the spring, I said, "Hell, Gus, you didn't have to send me that buck."

He grunted. "I don't want to owe nobody nuttin."

Ted Dew and Gus had always been good friends. They'd cut timber together, and Ted was an accomplished woodworker himself. Shortly after we came up from Beverly Hills to our new house, Ted stopped by and said, "You know, old Gus ain't feeling too well any more. That little place of his hooks into the ranch. I don't know if he'd sell it, but you'd be better off having it than somebody else."

I drove up to see Gus, arriving about four-thirty in the afternoon. He opened the door a crack, squinted at me. "I'm eating," he grunted.

"Well, can I come in?"

He shrugged diffidently. But it always began like this. You couldn't break in on him; and then, two hours later, you couldn't get away.

Gus was naked except for an old tattered pair of trousers. I soon understood why. The wood stove was flamed up hot and that cabin must have been a hundred degrees. Gus motioned me brusquely to a chair, and I sat with him. He was gnawing at a breaded whitefish; he also had one large leaf of lettuce on the oilcloth of his table. As we talked, he'd dunk the leaf into a cup of water, take a bite out of it, then lay it back on the oilcloth.

From time to time he'd forget who I was, that I had Ted Dew's old ranch down below him. Then he'd drift off into some story about the past which miraculously would hook up to Ted and I guess me. After nearly an hour, I came out with my business. I knew the homestead was his whole life, but he was getting to be an old man; he ought to think about his last years. I'd known that occasionally now he'd leave in the winters, go down and camp in the mountains of Arizona. I proposed to him that I buy the homestead and the buildings for five thousand dollars, and he live there the rest of his life.

"Dese goddamn cattle dey run in here," he barked, "dey knock my fences apart, knock down my wood animals in de yard, dey crap on my rocks. You got cattle too."

"We wouldn't have them bothering you, Gus, I promise you that."

"Anyhow," he grunted, "I don' wanta sell."

After another hour I wormed out of him that he had one heir, a brother back East someplace. He was sure the brother would want the homestead. "Then will you do this, Gus?" I asked. "Write your brother, tell him you've got a firm cash offer; ask him if he wants the place?"

Gus grunted around a bit more, finished the lettuce leaf. "Maybe I write him someday," he said, shrugging. "I pretty damn busy now."

When I left, I looked in the little window. Gus had a long box in which he kept volumes of *Reader's Digest,* mostly from the thirties and forties. He'd just taken one out, and was sitting by the searing stove, sweating and reading.

Several weeks passed. I'd learned enough by now not to go back and see Gus. But I worried too. Good pasture and river land were hard to find. People were always looking for loose pieces. Then about noon one day I happened to glance across the sagebrush and saw Gus bumping along in his old truck. Teddy didn't want me to interrupt my lunch, but I just had a feeling I ought to go out and see him.

I walked across the sagebrush and waited for his truck; we

133

visited a bit and then I said, casually, "Say, Gus, did you ever hear from your brother?"

He frowned, with a twinkle in his eye. "Just today . . . get de letter." He pointed at the corner of an envelope which he'd stuck beneath his leg on the seat.

"Well, what did he say?"

"By Got, I don't know yet. I just got it a couple hours ago."

"When you find out," I said, "I'd be . . . oh, kind of interested in hearing."

"I pretty damn busy. Sometime, I got time, I see you."

Another week. My city instinct said: Rush up to his cabin, get the answer. No, I just watched the cow trail north across the sagebrush, and finally, Gus's truck did appear. He drove as close to one mph as you could get, for the poor old truck couldn't stand much more. This time I leaned into the window. "How about it, Gus?"

He shrugged. "I sell da place, yah. Brother don' want it."

I was overjoyed. But Gus, I could see, was preoccupied. He was doing some carpentry at a nearby ranch. There were papers to be drawn up, a visit to a lawyer. Most of all, if we had a deal we'd better get it done before anybody changed his mind. I explained this to Gus.

"Ain't no hurry," he said. "I got too much work. Maybe couple of weeks I come by."

"Let's say Monday," I said. (This was Friday.)

He blew a long breath and stared at the sagebrush. I knew we were at the critical moment; the decision couldn't be put off any more. He knew it too, that grand old man. "Yah," he sighed, "mebbe Monday, okay. I be here eight o'clock."

I'd heard so many stories about buying land, about these old-timers who just couldn't let go. After all, it was their life. And Gus would have all weekend to think it over; I doubted if he'd come. But at seven-fifty Monday morning his truck creaked along the cow trail. He never would pull right up next to our house, so I walked again through the sagebrush and met him.

It was a fascinating two and half hours I spent on the way to the attorney's office in Rock Springs. Gus talked about the West as he'd known it. He was writing his memoirs, there in my station wagon. When he'd first made this trip from Rock Springs to Pinedale, he'd gone in a jerk-line freight wagon; took them fourteen hours to travel a hundred miles. He pointed out the stops they used to make, the old springs, the cow camps. He told me some of the men who had died. One, in the winter, was tracking over a pass he'd known all his life; a howling ground blizzard caught him. He couldn't see, the snow whipping up, bitter cold. He walked in circles for hours until his strength was gone. Then he lay down, put his pack under his head, folded his arms across his breast. That was how they found him, frozen to death less than a mile from the cabin of a friend.

In the lawyer's office, we read aloud the agreement of terms, and that Gus should live on the place for the rest of his life. Gus frowned at the papers and his eyes filled up. The lawyer handed him a pen.

"I don' think I can sign," Gus said. "Dis here elbow of mine it pops loose..." He then demonstrated that there was no possible way for him to get his signing hand down to the paper.

The lawyer said, "Well, I can sign for you, Gus."

"Oh? Is dat legal?"

"Yes, with witnesses."

Gus cleared his throat. "No, by Got, I going to sign the damn thing. Come dis far, didn't I?"

Then, with his blue eyes glistening wet, he scrunched and strained around, his fingers gripping the pen like an ax until he had scrawled in big jiggly letters: "August C. Galinat." Original deed from the United States Government, Woodrow Wilson, President.

Gus sniffled a bit and we all shook hands. Then the lawyer said, "Gus, if you're ever in town, drop in and see me. Like to visit with you."

Gus was beaming now. "Mister," he said, "with all dis money I got, dis fortune, I ain't gonna see nobody no more. Just looking out at beyond."

The lawyer and I glanced at each other as Gus stumped off down the hall. There wasn't anything to say except, maybe, good-bye to men like that. They weren't around "no more."

When we got back to the ranch that afternoon, Gus was silent. I knew he'd go back to his cabin and consider what he'd done. So I wanted to make it easy for him. "Gus," I said, "as far as I'm concerned, nobody has to know I've bought this land. You'll be living there just as always. We won't say a word. No embarrassment to you, explaining to the neighbors."

He pondered, then a rasp began deep in his chest. "I tink what we do"—he chuckled—"we tell everybody. All dem guys push cows in on me all dese years. We tell 'em. We rub de sonsofbitches' nose in it!"

As he got back into his truck, Teddy came out and begged him to come in, see our new house. "I've asked you so many times to have a meal with us, Gus," she said. "Please, won't you stay?"

He looked at the house, and at us. His bright blue eyes stared right through Teddy. "If I come in dis time," he grunted, "den I want to come back some more. Pretty soon, I get spoilt. Tanks, but I stay up home."

He never did come for a meal. He trudged up into the timber to cut more poles for his buck fence. But it was ours now. I tried to pay him. He'd take no money. He bought a new flame-red truck, went out for two winters camping on the Colorado River. He bought a cap down in Arizona, the kind that the retired folks wear out at Sun City. But beyond this, Gus remained consistent to his Spartan life. As time passed, he began to get what he called "crazy spells." I tried to take him to the doctor, but he said, "Nah, I get over dem. It is de sun. Pretty hot now for September. Remind me of one time here . . ."

In October some neighbors were moving cows down the trail leading past Gus's cabin. But when the head end of the cows reached there, they snorted and trotted wide. The cowboy sent one of his daughters riding over. She found Gus lying under his buck fence, dead for two days.

From Gus, I think, I learned the secret of these old-timers here, and perhaps the frontier too. They would do it the hard way because that was the only way they'd known. It was the necessary way for their survival. To give in to luxury for a moment would be, as he'd said, "to get spoilt." That's why you ran an elk to the top of the mountain, why you never quit or gave in to your human frailty when all the violence of the world seemed to be against you. You never owed anybody anything. You were your own man.

And Wells Robertson, too, was the same. Now, in the spring when we moved into our new house, I thought again about Wells. He would have been astounded by it, and yet it's a simple box of a house. But Wells would see the man-hours and the anguished cost of materials. Because, like Thoreau, Gus and Wells could build their own house with an ax on a mountainside; or failing that, lie out under a tree and sleep protected by the rhythm of the world they knew. And that we, too often, no longer can hear.

When Wells finally left us in Wyoming, he went back, as he said he would, to Rock Creek. Work to do, mining up in the red ledges. He had no money except for his meager World War I pension. The owner of the Rock Creek place still paid him nothing, but did let him squat and mine. Eventually, in a later winter, Wells must have run out of peanut butter and carrots. They found him down on the Indian reservation beside his jeep. He was naked, starving, and out of his mind. Neighbors rushed him to the state hospital, but by the time I got the news, Wells had died of exposure and pneumonia.

I saw Wally Young, his sidekick, once more . . . in a tough little coal-town saloon in Utah. Wally was coughing awful bad. "Aw hell," he said, "there ain't nothing the matter with me. Once when I was thirteen, I had an appendicitis. Know damn well that's what it was. But my Paw was cowboying and gone, wasn't no way for me to get fifty miles to town, or get a Doc out either, horses all gone. So Maw she said, 'Can't help you, sonny. You'll just have to get over it.' Well, I did, you know. Just like I'll get over this little cough. And we'll be up to see your new place on the Green, Willie and me. Now that Wells is gone."

Now that they're all gone.

But not quite.

Maybe, finally, some of it had rubbed off on me. I still have log gates Wells had made, and buck fences up at Gus's that I copied. These men could use an ax; I can barely use a gas saw. But I resolved to build a buck fence around our new house that might please even them. A buck fence is two notched logs set as a triangle, with three long poles connecting to the next buck. And the fence I finally made after weeks of labor, the old-timers would have chuckled at, creaky bucks and funny angles. But somehow it was a thing I did by myself, and when you're as helpless at carpentry as I am, I felt it connected me, in effort at least, to those men I loved.

Then with tractor, blade and hydraulic bucket, I landscaped our barren knoll overlooking the Green. Again, out here, nobody does it for you, and our two houses on the bluff, naked of trees, cried out for a lawn and flowers. In fact, my brother Pete took to calling the place Fort Carney, jutting up lonely in the sagebrush. All we needed was a bugler and a flag to put us back into the nineteenth century.

The time had come to take stock.
We had a new house and an unsold
one in Beverly Hills. I had no book to
write, no television either. When you've
spent most of your life writing, inactivity
galls you; you feel sterile, worthless. I knew
this was responsible for much of the trouble I
was having. I'd painted myself into a corner in my
two worlds, and I couldn't seem to extricate myself
satisfactorily from either.

**12**

The ranch was not making money. Dave Shannon and
I had tried everything we knew: increased the herd, killed and
beat sagebrush for better grass. But we were up against the ancient adversary, climate. I'd never been at the ranch during the
spring for calving. But now I saw it first-hand. The meadows
were still slushy with snow and ice. Teddy and I would drive out
in the Snow Cat, making the nightly rounds that Dave always
did. In sleeting hail we'd come on a fresh calf, wet in afterbirth
and still smoking from the heat of the mother's womb. We'd play
the headlights of the Snow Cat over him and watch his struggle
for life. He had to get up and suck at least once, and if he did, the
chances were that he'd live. But those that were born in the cold
nights would lie shivering, the mother cow licking, nudging.
Sometimes we'd get out of the Snow Cat and prop the little thing
up on his wobbly legs, point him at the udder. But these were the
calves we saw. Many others we'd find too late; they'd been born
sometime in the night and were already frozen into the ice-
sheeted ground. Others were humped up with scours, a form of
dysentery that can be fatal. Two more we found had been born,
of all places, directly beside a badger hole; they'd slid into it and
suffocated. Once a cow's calf dies, her tits swell up with unused
milk. At the same time, you may have another calf whose mother
won't nurse it, because her udder has been burned by the sun
reflecting on the snow; she's so sore-titted she refuses the calf and
bums him, as they say. So now we'd take the bummed calf and
cut the hide off the dead calf, fit it over the bum like a coat. Then
we'd plant him in front of the mother who needed to be nursed.
Again a drama. She'd sniff him, walk around him, snort at us.
Some cows you can fool this way, others you can't. But if she was
sufficiently fooled, she'd bump him with her udder and he'd be-

139

gin to suck. You had to watch him, though, because the hide you'd grafted on would overheat him, give him pneumonia in the severe climate. If you took the hide off too soon, the mother would realize it wasn't her calf and would bum him. If you took it off too late, he'd get sick and often die.

In these night and morning runs in the meadows, I began to understand my cows and the challenge they were pitted against in this climate and altitude. The corn feeders back in the Midwest loved these calves because they were healthy and very light, about 350 pounds when we sold them. They'd gain beautifully on somebody's corn and be worth a lot of money. But for us here, there just weren't enough total dollars in the calf. We had to breed them too late to avoid spring storms, so they never had a chance to grow up into profitable selling weights. We had to feed the mother cow two tons of hay over the winter, or about $40 against a $100 calf.

Like most city people, I'd always considered the cow a stupid, unfeeling beast. But not so with these high-country Wyoming range cows. They're angrily protective of their calves, and often will butt hell out of you if you try to touch one. And if you drag a dead calf away, they'll follow you and bawl in a mourning that almost makes you cry. Turn a range cow out in the upper pastures and she can tell by instinct when winter is coming. She'll drift down with her calf and stand at the gate, waiting to go home. A horse will run up a mountain, pawing snow to find new feed, and often starve. But a range cow will go downhill, home where she belongs. And out in the meadows with their newborn calves, the cows apparently have an understanding about predators and danger. You'll see perhaps twenty or thirty calves gathered around one old cow. Where are the other mothers? They're in the willows feeding or drinking. But they always leave a babysitter with the calves, and pity the coyote that would try to come in and steal one.

But for all the instinct of these cows, they couldn't fight the inflationary marketplace. They just cost too much to run here in the deep snow. But as I read the accounts of old-timers in this country, I realized they never tried to calve out where we did. They'd summer up here, use the rich grass; then they'd trail their cows far to the south on the desert, where they could be wintered cheaply. In fact, the old-timers never put up hay except for horses. But the blizzard of 1889 changed that. Early accounts told that from our ranch to Rock Springs, a hundred and twenty miles south, you could almost walk over the cattle carcasses, the loss was so great. Then, too, when the open range was fenced in, the trail drives ended; you needed permits to winter on the desert. Slowly it evolved that people began calving out and feeding hay even in the snow-country ranches.

There was an old cowboy working on the ranch next to me, and I discussed it with him. He said, "Right here is the finest yearling grass in the United States. A feller ought to get rid of this haying business and pasture yearlings on these river bottoms and hills. Grass is the cheapest asset you got."

Another cheap asset we had was labor: Tom, John, Pete and their friends, who each summer were standing in line to get haying jobs with us. But I knew this bonanza was going to end quite soon: the boys off in college; they could get better jobs out in the world and I wanted them to. If we did convert the ranch to yearlings, we wouldn't have to put up hay; we could pasture our meadows. But, as a cow buyer told me, "This yearling business is the biggest crap game you'll ever play in." You had to buy them at inflated prices in the spring, hope to get a good gain and pray for prices to hold in the fall. Both Dave Shannon and my older brother Bill, who's a good businessman, were against the yearling proposition. Yet I was still bothered by the ranch losing money. I bought a few yearlings in the summer to try them out.

As for writing, the failure of *The Monroes* and the brain book hit me hard. I spent hours in my new office, staring out the window, trying to find what I wanted to write next. And I went back, too, and looked over *The Monroes*. Originally I'd started with a dramatization of the frontier I felt I knew here. You do see a dream when you first get an idea. But the rub is, you can never quite translate it in its original beauty. I'd particularly had this trouble in the film medium. What I saw, directors, actors and others didn't see the same way: practical considerations entered, other egos became involved. Often, too, I realized, I didn't have the filmic skills to crystallize an idea into one line or one action that summarized a scene as succinct as a telegram. But 20th Century Fox or ABC must necessarily be business machines. They flailed and ate any writer's material as it came to them. Like a tractor going downhill, if it veers from the driver's prescribed course, the tractor doesn't feel. You've got to use muscle and argument to get it back going straight. I've never been very good at creative shout-downs; but to succeed in the studios you must be stubbornly superconfident, steamroll over the opposition and cling to your original course. You have to learn to fight against the organization, and hence much of your creative energy is spent in protecting your back. I saw this as a waste of time.

So I couldn't blame Fox or ABC. I simply didn't have the brass for their kind of war. Too often I'd swallowed my own instincts, and now they had to come up. Yet the fact still remained that I'd pretty well cut myself off from the film world. The original creation of prose gives you the independence I seemed to demand. But where was the prose now? I wrote page after page of diaries, ideas for stories, but none seemed to spark me. My confidence was gone. I was not a bit sure I'd ever write again.

But when you stop blindly pursuing one goal, you do, I think, begin to see things you never had time to look at before. I particularly noticed the change in myself when my old friends from the cities would come out to fish or hunt. They'd arrive highly keyed, ready for the chase; they'd set up their rods or guns and off we'd go. They'd plunge into the sport with numbers as the goal, symbols. Often, in the gray dawn, I'd awaken to voices on the river below our bedroom. I'd peer out foggily, and there would be some of my pals, flinging lures and snapping flies. Their breaths would be steaming in the frost. I'd holler at them, "Hey, the trout won't bite now. You've got to get some sun on the water. Come in and have breakfast. Relax."

But it was hard for them to relax, and God knows I didn't blame them for that syndrome. They were determined to jam every moment with action before they flew back to the city and the Big Game. An old part of me envied their competitiveness; and the new part sometimes felt sad because, compared to their glittery, much recompensed lives, mine seemed pretty simple.

I noticed, too, that I was beginning to have new feelings about wildlife. I no longer regarded them as quarry but as intimates. In the beaver ponds and on the river, I'd come to know where certain large trout lived. Their habits fascinated me; I could tell their moods. I'd watched them fight the seasons and raise their young; indeed, Davy Shannon and I had trapped small trout, lugged them on our backs in milk cans through sagebrush to plant new ponds. I'd watched the duck broods grow, seen coyote and skunk rob their nests. One ill-advised Canada goose laid her eggs atop a haystack; we had to feed the hay, so we removed the eggs and only a couple hatched. When you live enough with wild game, you come to realize what a miracle their survival is. Surely some must be taken by hunters and fishermen, but I wanted that taking appreciated. And when I fished myself, if I had a large one on I'd fight for him, just as I used to, but all the others I'd release. I have a few trophies on my walls; they're enough.

Of more value to me were the precious moments I'd been able to share the wild world. For instance, one day at the beaver ponds I was squatting in the sagebrush, engrossed in tying on a fly. I happened to glance up. Across the pond, a few yards away, a superb brown bear and her twin cubs were drinking. They hadn't seen or winded me. I watched them, their fur rippling in the sun, the mother communicating with the cubs in nuzzles and nudges. Finally, when I stood up and identified myself, she snorted and stared at me. But there was no fear in the look. They finished drinking, then glanced at me with almost a shrug and walked slowly back up into the timber.

Or, another day when we were riding for cows, there were antelope springing up in the sagebrush. Then the cattle dogs sped off barking, running down a baby antelope, a tiny wobbly thing not much bigger than a rabbit. Davy Shannon grabbed it and put it on his saddle. When he got home he and Dave built a pen. They named the young female Agnes, fed her on a bottle. Well, Agnes grew and prospered. She got so tame she'd eat grain out of your pocket; she'd come in the house. She was as affectionate as a dog, and she grew up with the cows and calves, spent the winter eating hay with them. But then, in the summer, we moved the cows and calves to the upper pastures. Suddenly Agnes was alone, hanging around our houses and sheds. She was lost. Obviously, she'd thought of herself as a calf. Soon, though, the antelope herds began moving up into the grasslands. Agnes would drift farther toward them each day. Finally she didn't come home for her grain; she'd gone to the herd. That fall, when the antelope moved down to lower country, Agnes again came near the houses. We'd call to her; she'd stop and watch us. For several days she hung around; then one dusk I saw her trotting south after her mates. She'd made up her mind what she was.

But she came back the next spring. She had twin fawns; when we'd ride near her, call her name, she'd stand and not run off with the herd. She remembered us just enough to let us get close; then she'd drift away.

To me now, in the changing tempo, all the animals became identities, friends. One day up in the timber it'd be a family of ruffed grouse chicks trotting after their mother. I love to shoot and eat grouse: but these helpless little things? I asked myself. By autumn, though, my mercy would have passed. Hunt for hours, climb over enough deadfalls, and you realize that the grouse are more than a match for man. When I'd finally put them up in a roar of wings, I'd take one. My Lab, Sheba, would look at me mournfully as if to say, "What's the matter with you? I've gone to all this trouble of finding them, let's get the rest."

Some other day, I thought. Because there was time now, and in it an understanding I hadn't had before.

But if I was communicating happily with animals that summer, I'm not sure how well I was doing with people. We had, over the years, made quite a few friends among the various ranchers. We were beginning to belong to Pinedale . . . but that word has a far different connotation here than in Beverly Hills. Our valley, unlike the Jackson or Sheridan area, has not been infiltrated by outsiders. It's a clannish land where the ranches have been owned by the same families almost since homesteading. These people are not quick to accept newcomers; they don't have anything against them; they treat you well but they hold their distance. And social life, particularly during the summers, is almost nonexistent. It has to be: everyone is simply too damn busy. For the average rancher, social life is a branding party, a rodeo, or going off neighboring. The women and men usually take to different sides of the room, talk cows, tell stories, and that's that. Sometimes the men go to sleep in the grass or with their head propped in a corner of a cabin. Teddy and I were truly impressed by these people, we enjoyed their company, but we knew that it would be years, if ever, before we could be received as one of them.

But our boys, meanwhile, were getting involved in the community. With local friends they'd organized a rock band called

144

The Missing Link. They played in the Pinedale church hall and sometimes down at Big Piney on Saturday nights. Because there's only one movie theater in the county, the local kids were ripe for entertainment and they turned out in droves. Soon, to the boys' amazement, The Missing Link was announced on the radio as a local news item. They began advertising the dances in store windows. The customers paid a dollar each and got their hands stamped. Sometimes the lads would make forty or fifty dollars apiece for a Saturday night's work.

To head off any possible trouble at these wing-dings, the sheriff suggested we have a rotating group of chaperons. Teddy and I did several stints at the blast-outs. They were exactly that. The kids had monstrous amplifiers on their guitars, plus a microphone for the singer. Tom's drums would thunder; John and Pete shouted songs together, the vocals of which I still haven't heard; then their friends from our hay crew would join them on chorus. During haying season many outsiders came up to work in the fields. The sheriff's car would cruise around the hall to make sure the drinks were still soft and nobody was getting pummeled in the alley.

One night, while we were chaperoning the din, I noticed an unkempt hay-hand kid wearing jeans and a dirty sweatshirt. I'm six feet three and he must have stood six, six. But he wasn't standing very well; he had a bottle hidden someplace and was trying to start fights in the hall. With no great enthusiasm, I could see that the chaperon duty now required bouncing. I approached the kid and told him he'd have to leave. I had, through some foresight, steeled my fingers into his big shoulder. To my amazement, he followed like a lamb and I led him out. Then it dawned on him; he started to flail drunkenly, muttered he was going for his buddies, come back and wreck the joint.

Get the sheriff, somebody said, and that was the best suggestion so far. Meanwhile, the kid was trying to steal my truck or anybody's; fortunately, the keys were gone. So was the sheriff. I wandered up and down the main street looking for him, but the saloons were ablaze and there was enough of the traditional Saturday night fisting to occupy the sheriff elsewhere. On my return to the hall, a neighbor's kid came running up. "Mr. Carney," he cried, "the big guy's back, on the fight. He's a-looking for you."

145

It was beginning to sound like *High Noon*. But just as I approached the showdown, the highway patrolman's car swerved in. At the same time Dave Shannon arrived to pick up his daughters. The big hay-hand took a wild boozy swing, knocked the patrolman down. Dave jumped the kid, I scrambled for his legs, and he fell like a sack of hops. The patrolman brushed himself off and put cuffs on.

After *The Monroes* fights, it was an awful letdown: tame as real life, you might say. The poor kid apparently had spent some time in reform school and now he got a couple of days to dry out and repent in the Pinedale jail. When I came back into the hall, I tried to tell Teddy the outcome.

"What?" she shouted, cupping her ear.

Then we grinned and looked at The Missing Link, vibrating their deafening beat. You couldn't have heard the FBI machine-gunning Bonnie and Clyde in that hall. By the small hours of the morning the kids would come out from town, count their money and split it up. At eight A.M. they'd be in the hay meadows, bucking those god-awful bales.

Dave said that summer, "There ain't a hay crew in the valley as good as ours." I think he was right.

Haying, that cruel medieval torture, is a team operation. You've got to have élan, a controlled anger to conquer the fields, beat the weather, win. Several of our boys were regulars, coming back year after year for wages of about five dollars per day, depending on ranch finances, usually bankrupt by August. These kids proved themselves superbly, running tractors, maintaining machinery, and most of all, caring about doing the job right.

During haying our John was up at six A.M. and gone. He was the mowing man, speeding his tractor out into the bottoms, sharpening his sickles, racing time so he'd always be ahead of the crew. Later, when the dew had dried, the boys would hook up the wagons that worked behind the baler. Some crews leave the bales in the field overnight, but they get damp this way. Ours were hoisted onto the wagons as they left the baler. Tom and Pete worked on the stacks, fitting the bales into the log cribs, tromping down the corners. The stacks would rise a good thirty feet above the ground, the kids dancing on the bales and fitting them with all the surefootedness of Indian steelworkers, high above some city. Nobody ever fell off. Indeed, they had learned to jump down from the stacks and not get hurt. The crews usually divided into two teams and they'd race each other for the best production. At noon Teddy, Carmen and I would come out to the field in the truck. Teddy would serve full-course meals—turkey, ham—and bring a picked carcass home. She baked her own bread, rolls, two pies a day, a bucket of mashed potatoes, but we never filled those kids.

Also in the truck we'd bring out guitars. For a half hour we'd lie in the sweet-smelling grass, and The Missing Link, gratefully without amplifiers, would harmonize on ballads. Some our John had written himself, and Pete, also a guitarist now, had a fine voice to accompany him. They played their specialties: "Draft Dodgers Rag," "Plastic Jesus," "Lizzie Borden," "Sloop John B."

Then they'd get up, yawning and mock-protesting about going back to work; but they loved it, really, loved the challenge. In the afternoons thunderclouds would build. Often I'd sit in my office and watch, across the river, the deadly whips of lightning crackling toward the stacks and the crew in the field. Then I'd see Peter doing an Indian rain dance on top of the stack, praying it to come his way. But if it did, Dave always seemed to know just how much time they had. John would shut off his mowing tractor and run for the willows, then the other kids would be scrambling down into the protection of the cribs. In all the years of giving these kids hard dangerous jobs, we'd only had one injury, a boy who happened to trip when he was timbering and cut his knee with his ax.

The afternoons seemed interminable. Occasionally I'd buck a few bales, just to show how old I was. I'd hurt my back long ago when a horse fell on me, and now my disks winced at every eighty-pound bale. More often I'd watch the kids in the distance, see the stacks rising. It would get to be seven, then eight o'clock, the shadows lengthening, and they were still out there. I computed, watching them one afternoon, that at the rate they were going, each boy was lifting by hand 27,000 pounds, thirteen and a half tons each day. And still, when I'd see the trucks and tractors start for home, here came some of the hay crew running! No, not even running. They were sprinting, across the bridge, up the last half-mile to the house. Our John could always outstrip them because he was the track man. But Tom, when he came to our gate, would fling out his arms in a hammed-up tape-breaking gesture for the photographer. "Don't you guys know when you've had enough?" I said. "What the hell are you doing?"

"Getting ready for football."

Too soon (not for them but for me) the haying was over. I rather suspected then that we were coming to the end of an era. We'd hayed for five years now, but if I had the courage to go to yearlings, these magnificent crews weren't going to be needed any more. When I said goodbye to them and wrote their checks that September, I got a lump in my throat. These kids had passed through us, through the picnics and The Missing Link and the days up timbering fence posts: worked like hell, burned a lot of my gas chasing girls hundreds of miles; ate out the larder. But having them was our privilege. The present generation may be going to hell, as the politicians say, but I didn't see it here. These kids were so much more mature and responsible than I'd ever been at their age, I wished I could have started over and been them for these few years.

When we shipped off our boys that fall, they seemed to have turned a corner. After the years of Utah and Wyoming, they were men now—sunburned, hard-handed, self-reliant. They were also strange mixtures—blue jeans, worn-out cowboy boots and tweed coats and ties. These latter had been put on for Grandmother, because they'd pass through Chicago on their way East.

The boys were inseparable, as if the shared experience and isolation of ranch life had forged them into one. They hated to leave each other, and we them. Our long-distance phone bills were going to be staggering. But I did see a growing independence in the kids now. It had been a gamble, tearing them away from "home" in Beverly Hills, making them put on this new life. The test lay ahead for all of us: Had it worked? Could we live with it?

Teddy and I stayed at the ranch until we sold the cattle. I particularly wanted to see the results of my small yearling experiment. When we weighed the hundred yearling heifers, I found they'd made satisfactory gains and netted us about $2,000. This seemed better than calves, but I postponed the decision of converting to yearlings until the following spring. I hoped by then that I'd have the answers to some bigger problems in my life.

Teddy and I drove leisurely back to Los Angeles. After being

148

away seven months, I wasn't particularly looking forward to getting there: I had no book to write, no prospects in TV. More than this, we'd be rattling around alone in our big house: Tom and Pete gone; and John, it seemed, had been away for a hundred years. It was going to be different now. Then Teddy quoted a bit of wisdom that my Aunt Frances had told her. Franny had advised her family . . . and she had seven kids: "Look, I want you to understand that your father and I started out together and we're going to end together. You kids are just passing through . . ."

As Teddy said, "It's our life now. They're started, they're on the road. It's time we begin to think of what we want."

She couldn't have made this statement at a better moment. We were then just lifting over the hills of the L.A. basin, coming in on the San Fernando Freeway. I tried, momentarily, to look for the Panorama City of our first California Christmas. I couldn't find it. The entire valley was blanketed in yellow, acrid smog. The place was burning up, brush fires in the hills, traffic racing, cutting in around us. I glanced ahead toward the Santa Monica mountains: how often, making this drive, I'd been hurrying to get up into the cool hills of Benedict Canyon. But now it seemed like somebody else's home. After the peaceful green world we'd left, the tire-squealing, anxious chase here struck me as senseless, repugnant. "Who needs this?" Teddy said.

Our actor and actress tenants were very attractive young people. They also had a good future in show business. They ought to have a house like ours, and I suggested this to them when we came into our living room that afternoon.

Ryan O'Neal agreed that they'd really loved the place. But they weren't quite ready to buy anything yet. They would, however, continue to rent it if I wanted to extend the lease.

"No," I said, "we've rented it long enough. I really want to get out."

Before we could resettle ourselves in the Beverly Hills house, Teddy and I decided on the spur of the moment to fly to New York. I was hoping to talk to publishers, get a feel of the book business. I was so unproductive I needed some affirmation that there was still an "old writer's" audience out there. My publishers assured me that there were indeed a surprising amount of people who wanted to read a good story in the traditional sense.

They agreed that there was a lot of gimmicky stuff around, sex-ploitation and youth appeal. I couldn't write these any more than change my skin. But what did I want to write? Someday soon, I answered, I'm going to know. And that was almost a prayer.

Then, on a weekend, for the first time in twenty-four years, I went back down to Princeton. Walk on Prospect Street, see a few faces, memories. What a shock that was. I didn't know the place. When I used to ride the milk trains back from New York, I could say in my sleep the litany of station stops. Now many of these hamlets were transformed into vast tract cities; Princeton was a big traffic-jammed commuting town with a fringe of factories and think-tanks out where we used to shoot ducks.

But it was good to see the past departed. People were having damn few debut parties any more where girls fell down stairs. The eating clubs, where I'd made so many lasting friends, were on the wane, considered undemocratic. I didn't mourn the change. The kids were overdue a world of their own.

In a soggy rain outside of Palmer Stadium, I watched Tom playing defensive halfback for the Yale freshmen. He'd had a good season, as had John, who was also a halfback at Portsmouth Priory. The following Saturday we saw John score two touchdowns. Then we went up to New Hampshire to watch Pete. He was co-captain of his reserve team. As his coach said, "He's not exactly the best player out there, but he's really got authority. He runs this squad."

We had one night together with all the boys in New Haven. Their football seasons were over, their moment of glory done. Far more important to me was the progress they'd made. It seemed a long way back to the little cabin in Utah, the capguns, racing the horses, staging the Olympics. But for all the chaos of our life in the last few years, they'd survived, even profited. I felt then that our gamble had worked. They were on their own.

On an afternoon in February 1968, I sniffed the bloom of freedom and thought it was mine for all time. There was a young woman outside, admiring the bougainvillaea. Then she began to run like a schoolgirl down the driveway, holding her husband's hand. I said to Teddy, "They're it. They're going to buy."

# 13

Within a week, they had: actress Ann-Margret and her producer-husband, Roger Smith. Almost before we'd left the house, they'd made plans for remodeling it. There was talk that they were going to put up posters of Humphrey Bogart, turn the bar into a Bogart Room. I think he would have liked that. I don't know whether Hedy Lamar and Bob Newton got their memorial chambers too; I've never been back to see. However, I did notice recently, in the Los Angeles *Times,* Ann-Margret's appraisal of the house. "Seven acres of seclusion," she said, "reached only by a steep and somewhat shoddy road angling off Benedict Canyon, high in the hills of Beverly. It's my escape hatch, my hideaway, my home. My husband, Roger Smith, and I can get lost there . . . lost in the peace and quiet . . ."

Join the club, Ann. But when we drove down the driveway, following the moving truck, we didn't look back. By then spring was supposed to be coming to Wyoming. I'd loaded up bird dogs, pots and pans for the last shuttle trip, and we went home to Cora, population three.

The final breaking with California was obviously difficult: we'd left a lot of ourselves there, but I didn't realize it yet. Now that we had money in our pockets and quite a frugal way of life up in the sagebrush, we decided it was time to blow the boys to a Grand Tour. We flew to New York, picked them up, and had a roaring goodbye party on the boat. We were on the *Bremen,* going to Europe, three weeks of Kultur for our hay hands who'd never been any place. There was a lot to shout about: Tom had finished his first Yale year with honors, football, baseball, and working on the Yale *Record.* John had captained his track team, set a record for victories; the school awarded him the sportsmanship prize, and he'd gained early acceptance into Stanford. Meanwhile, cool-cat Pete not only passed all his courses but had turned into

151

a fine skier and was elected Keeper of the Spirit, head rooter for the school.

We drank to all of them, then plunged eastward to France, basked on a beach in Spain and visited with friends in England. The last leg of the trip was Ireland; I wanted the boys to see where their great-grandfather had come from. "Know your roots," I had said in my best tour-guide manner. "See who you are." Little did I dream I'd be the one finding out.

My grandfather had emigrated from County Mayo in the 1860's. Now we were driving across the rocky land on a drizzling day, arriving at a little Gaelic town just in time to see a livestock sale in progress. There were hundreds of Irishmen in the village square; they'd come in pickup trucks, jaunting carts. They were bartering in Gaelic, one fellow in a soggy tweed cap squeaking out a tune on a violin. Everywhere sheep were bleating, swine squealing, a calf breaking loose, kids chasing him through the heaps of chicken crates.

It was too much of a party to miss; we stopped and I got talking with the farmers. Then an old man, peg-legged and a patch on one eye, hobbled up. "Malachy," one of the farmers said to him, "shake hands with a Yank by the name of Carney." He pronounced it "Kaaarney." "His people come from Laughra-sheen, he says."

"It was a way back," I explained.

"There's a helluva lot of Carneys, God help us," Malachy grunted.

"Misther Carney," continued another farmer, "has been looking at our calves here. He's a livestock man himself. Has a cattle ranch in the States. Where was that now?"

"Wyoming."

"Ah," somebody murmured. "Wyoming, out West. Must be a grand enormous place you have there."

I said no. It was pretty small by comparison. About twenty-six hundred acres.

"Jesus God."

By now Malachy, the old man, was squinting his one blue eye at me. He tapped me on the leg with his cane. "Is that your family you got with you, them there?" He nodded toward Teddy and the boys.

Yes, I said, they were my family. I added that we'd been

traveling around Europe, but this was the high point, County Mayo. I grinned, but Malachy was dour.

He pushed up his cap with his thumb. "Are you meaning to tell me you brought them all the way here, on the profits of livestock? It must be a helluva better business for you than us!"

"Well no," I said. "I surely couldn't pay for this on cows. I had a little cash put away . . ."

Malachy grunted and appeared satisfied. But then another farmer spoke up. "Why," he exclaimed, "I know about that Wyoming state you live in. It's the fierce moun-tainous place where the family come to on the telly. The Monroes, they call themselves. Didja see them now over there, misther?"

I looked at the grizzled faces, squinty eyes, jaws clamped on pipes. I might have made them believe the cow part of it, but oh brother, this too? "Well," I said, "I have seen the Monroes. Yes. As a matter of fact, I wrote them."

Slowly the pipes came out of teeth. The farmers gave little side glances at each other. "I . . . am also a writer," I added quickly. "Do some TV. I sort of outlined that Monroe series."

"Ah, for God's sake," somebody breathed. "Didja hear that, Malachy. You seen the telly with me one night. Him, himself! He wrote it!"

Malachy's one eye had narrowed down to the size of a rifle sight. He was staring right through me, then snorted as only an Irishman can, and went pegging away. Occasionally he'd glance over his shoulder, glower at me and shake his head. I could almost hear him muttering: Why, that goddamn lying Yank . . . another of them blatherskites . . . and to make it worse, with a Mayo name!

But there it was, exposed in a little town in Ireland: a rancher and a writer. Maybe I had to run all the way back here to my roots, to find who I was. You couldn't wipe out either of the worlds that were in you. You just had to learn to live with them both.

Now, cut adrift from the familiar in California, the job was up to me to make a new life in Wyoming. I got what you might call a jarring start. Two days after we'd come home from Europe, I went out to ride for cattle. A horse I'd had for over a year, and trusted, chose this moment to buck me ten feet in the air. I never got a hand under me, lit on my back and ached for days.

153

While I was still hobbling around, a representative from the state government paid me a call. He loved the Green River, as all of us did. But he told me now that definite plans were being made to put in the Kendall Dam that would wipe us out.

With some of my neighbors, I organized a group called The Save the Green Committee. Using all the facts I could garner from state and federal agencies, I wrote a detailed report, pointing out why the Kendall Dam would be a disaster, and recommending other possible sources of water that Wyoming felt it must have to industrialize the state. (Not that I was in favor of *that*, but the politicians apparently are. Gary, Indiana, on the Green!)

Banding together as we did, over a subject as ticklish as water, we made some enemies, but friends too. Our campaign picked up momentum and we began getting help from fishermen and citizens scattered across many states who loved the Green. Finally, public concern was aroused, not only for this river but for the ecology of the United States. In a period of two or three years, national attitudes changed about preserving the wildernesses. Yet, here in Wyoming, every time the legislature meets, the specter of the dam is raised again. All sorts of excuses are given by the politicians: unless we dam our water it will be stolen from us; or, we need the water to lure in the vast payrolls of industry which will exploit our coal, oil shale, and build odoriferous pulp mills. The politicians never seem to hear the ranchers in the back of the meeting halls, who say, "We like Wyoming the way it is. Let's put a fence around it." And so the fight goes on, and has become for many of us a challenge that grows in frustration, fascination, and still gives hope that if we fight hard enough, we may be able to preserve the freedom we know here for the generations beyond.

But still, no writer can be happy without his craft. Mine had been dead a long time. Yet now, I hoped, I could brew some of the past, mix it with my present feelings and come up with a book.

What I'd blundered onto was a fascinating, little-known era: 1916 on the Mexican border. The United States had sent General Pershing into Mexico with a Punitive Expedition, chasing Pancho Villa to punish him for his attack on Columbus, New Mexico. It was a hopeless, unpopular war, and also a moment of great change. Pershing had with him the first six airplanes we ever used in combat; the first trucks and also the last Apache Indian scouts who had been subjugated a few years earlier. As I saw it, the Mexican border war was a requiem for the frontier and the old cowboy philosophy: the beginning of United States involvement in the intrigues and blood baths of the modern world.

To dramatize it, I went all the way back to the cave in Utah and resuscitated none other than Sam Eagle. Now, as a Wyoming cowboy, working on a ranch in Mexico, Sam's adventure paralleled the Punitive Expedition, and during it, he came to see that his day was done.

In researching the book, I spent time in Arizona, New Mexico and the state of Chihuahua, where much of the Punitive Expedition took place. Because I speak passable Spanish, I not only dug up several old men who had ridden with Villa and Pershing, but I came on a new cattle country. There were yearlings all over Chihuahua. Some were being imported to summer grass in Wyoming. Suddenly I thought I'd found a solution for making the -E- pay. We'd buy Mexican cattle, lease or possibly buy a ranch in Arizona to hold them on until we were ready to come north with them in the spring.

On the strength of this idea, I sold our loyal cow herd, made a profit; we were now ready to convert to yearlings. Then winter set in, our first full winter in Wyoming. I went into shock. Talk about cabin fever . . . I felt like the Monroes' African lion, caged up in the howling snow of December, the phone dead for days, no mail. I hurried Sam Eagle to conclusion, and by late January, I was desperate to flee south, get the hell out of here. I had cattle lined up to look at, ranches, a manuscript to proof. Arizona was tennis courts, orange trees and even a plunge in the Pacific off Mexico.

On the morning we were ready to leave, the temperature dropped to thirty-nine below. I couldn't start our Snow Cat, which was going to lug our baggage across the bridge to where my car was parked, with its electric heater plugged in. So I began to shuttle belongings over by snow machine. I'd also taken the precaution of calling the county road crew, to be sure their snowplow would open us up. For days we hadn't seen the sun; now it was sparkling bright, revealing an arctic landscape, drifts eight and ten feet deep. "It's absolutely beautiful!" Teddy cried, digging in our luggage for the movie camera.

155

My reaction was: "Where in the hell is that snowplow?"

Our phone had blown out sometime in the night, so I finally raced over to the neighbor's, a couple of miles on a snow machine. It had now warmed up to twenty-one below. "By God, Otis," said the foreman at the county shop, "we ain't forgot you. It's just that we can't break through that road. At least, not without help. If you had a Cat . . ."

"I don't." /

"Well, I'm afraid you'll have to hire one to help us out, deep as it is."

More phone calls. Finally I located a private contractor's Cat. It was frozen solid. Not until late afternoon did they get it warmed up enough to start, hauled it out the long road. The Cat worked and chuffed into the sunset, pushing up the snow until only about twenty feet of glacier still blocked us. Then the Cat slid off the road and got stuck. That meant getting another neighbor with his Cat, chaining, groaning until the first one was free and they finally cut a tunnel for us. Teddy photographed this too in shivery Eastman Color. The tunnel through the drifts was higher than our car. By my schedule, we were due in Salt Lake that night. We barely made Pinedale. "Now do you see"—I glowered at Teddy—"why we can't winter cattle or people up in this damn place!"

We finally did get to Arizona, and had no luck in locating a ranch. Moreover, the Mexican yearling market was booming down there. We discovered that they cost as much on the border as we'd have to pay in Wyoming, then add the trucking. Nobody, least of all me, had figured out the answer for beating this game.

We arrived back in Wyoming on April Fool's Day. We'd found no ranch for wintering yearlings, had not bought yearlings, and the "little spring storms," as they called them, were still howling at the door. Only about a foot of snow left. Teddy hurried to put on her cross-country skis. I wanted to join her; we were tired and cramped from driving. But first I had a mountain of mail. Near the top was a letter from my publisher. We'd been through two books together. They were eagerly awaiting Sam Eagle.

I read the first line and caught my breath; a fine editor, a good friend: "This is one of the most difficult letters I've ever written . . ."

They didn't like Sam Eagle. Sorry. They were declining to publish it.

I took the letter out to Teddy. She was sitting in the front hall, buckling on her skis. "If they won't take it," I said, "nobody will. We should have bought cattle and lined up a place in Arizona, gone into the cow business for keeps. It's pretty obvious I'm not a writer any more."

"Don't say that!" she cried. "There are other publishers."

"Other books too. This one doesn't fit, and I can't write the ones that do."

We submitted Sam Eagle to several other houses, including one that had published three of my books. The reaction was unanimous: Sam Eagle didn't seem to have any present-day appeal; and, being a first draft, there were some obvious flaws in it. I knew that when I sent it off, but had hoped somebody would see enough promise in it to want to proceed.

There we were, home in Wyoming, skiing in April. The dizzy spells were back in Technicolor. I knew I'd hit the last low. Something had to change pretty quick, and God willing, give me the humility to have it be me.

Sense of worth, this was the poison in the blood. Indeed, maybe it's the sickness of our times, at least in many who were raised and trained as I. We've been nurtured on the creed that only by doing can we have fulfillment. Money, power, fame, get to the top: then you have self-esteem, because you're the mirror of what society adulates. But fail to make it . . . just "be" not "do" . . . just be committing daily to your life in all its aspects, accepting your failures and your blessings and continuing to commit, regardless of outcome: this is not the coin of success. "Be careful in nothing," said St. Paul. Go out and live fully. It doesn't matter whether you win or lose, just how you play the game.

What a dreadful old cliché!

And yet—is it? What else really does come to matter? Particularly now in a world that is so overamplified by media, confused, torn: a world of guilt, neuroses and the strivings of little men. Remember Finley Peter Dunne describing them: "Progress! Progress, oho! I can see th' stars winkin' at each other an' sayin: 'Ain't they funny! Don't they think they're playin' hell!' "

I thought I was.

But here on the quiet river, with a phone that doesn't work much, mail that seldom comes; no newspapers except on Sunday, one channel of TV that you don't watch . . . strange, you begin not to hear the sound of the game any more. By no means do you quit. You can't ever do that. But it somehow doesn't seem so important *what* you do, when it's just for yourself. You ride a horse and move some cows someplace, run a tractor, help a friend, build a lumpy bridge, but it's something you've done, you. The same for a daily page of a writer's journal; nobody'll ever read it, not even you again. But yet here for the first time, because there are no outside sounds, you can linger over the forked tail of a swallow, wonder how he flies; see the ripple of wind in the grass and rain dappling on still water. There's not a penny in it. But are you, for being you, feeling the richness of the world around you . . . are you any less worthy than a man who's running General Motors? Society tells you that you have no value. But God, I think, knows you do.

You have come finally to see how small and insignificant you truly are; and the moment you can admit and breathe that, that is the moment you begin a new life.

Stop caring about doing or what the world says. Be. Commit to being with all the ardor of your soul.

You can't put on a new philosophy like a nightshirt. There's another fellow in the bed; he's been there forty-some years and doesn't want to leave. He sneaks back in when you don't expect him. But now at least you know who he is, the damn thief who robs you of your authenticity. You kick him out again and again, until finally he comes back less often and even whimpering. Because you don't really have time for him any more. Something else has unfolded, a kind of what-the-hell-fling-the-chips creative freedom you've never known before. It leads you down strange corridors.

Mathematics, for instance.

Not me! I'm a writer.

But since I had nothing to write, and did have yearlings to buy, I found myself fascinated by the bog of mathematical equation you must go through on every purchase. A cattle dealer calls you and says, "I've got a load of 112 steers, weight 425, price 36¢, do you want 'em?"

"How the hell do I know?" I'd say. First I'd have to figure what each one costs per head, then the total dollars, what the interest would be for five months, trucking, ranch costs. Finally, I'd have to estimate what they'd gain, multiply that out to a suspected fall price and see whether I could afford to gamble on them. By this time I'd littered a page with multiplication, and wasn't too sure of my answers at that.

Then my brother Pete came out. He'd invented a slide rule for finding price times earnings in stocks. I said, "Why couldn't we do something like this for all livestock transactions? There are thousands of these trades being made every day, all over the country, guys sitting around auction barns, multiplying the same old figures out the long way on brown paper bags."

"Try it," Pete said.

"But I don't know anything about slide rules."

"In a half hour I'll tell you all there is."

It took more like six months. With Pete's patient help, I evolved what we copyrighted as the Cowputer, with the caption beneath it: "A Money Machine . . . computing the per head price of cattle, sheep or hogs. Showing your expenses, your gain and what you have to sell for to make a profit. A stockman's solace, removing surprise and sorrow at shipping day. Does everything but smile at your banker."

Well, the Cowputer won't pay for the ranch, but it's out, being advertised, and a few stockmen, cautiously suspicious of anything new—this is the first calculator ever used in the business—are beginning to buy it. So add to writer a mail-order salesman; and it's been fun, an education.

Slowly, too, there's come a sense of beginning to belong to the community. Organize a local chapter of Trout Unlimited to fight against dams and irresponsible timbering. Serve as a director of the Green River Cattleman's Association; rewrite a script for a local pageant, or a letter for the Mountain Man museum that would preserve the heritage of the fur traders who opened the West.

The challenges are different here, but you have time for them, time to make a speech to the fifth-grade class on conservation; fight for a road to be paved or better mail service; or haul a boatload of lost kids out of the river. Mundane things, but each is clearly an experience.

For instance, it seemed simple for Teddy to want to go to dinner and hear a traveling symphony in Rock Springs. It's just a 250-mile round trip; we do it often. So Teddy set her hair, put on a brand-new coat. Then in the late afternoon we walked out of the house into another "little spring storm." The Snow Cat had come up with a dead battery, so I perched Teddy behind me on a smaller snow machine. By this time of year the trails are hard-packed and crusted. With the blizzard in my face, I couldn't see, hit a ridge and catapulted Teddy into a snowbank. She landed rear-first with her hands still tucked in her new fur muff. The ranch road was a bog of ice and snow; we had to stop to open the gate. Teddy stepped through the ice around it and the slush sucked off her boot. We arrived at Rock Springs an hour late, splattered and wet, enjoyed a wonderful dinner party and concert. When we got back to the ranch, about two A.M., the road had blown in. The truck skidded off into a snowbank and we walked the rest of the way home. Teddy's eyes sparkled when she said, "Aren't we lucky to have good music and good friends so close?"

For the city man, though, at least this one, it takes a long time to slow down and truly hear the sound of a different drummer. And often the joys of it are not what you'd expect. Perhaps you even begin to reach people in ways you weren't aware of.

For instance, Pete recently invited a schoolmate to the ranch. Each year we get many letters from parents, asking us to take their kids, get them out of cities and "put 'em to work." Well, with haying gone, we don't have any need for our local Job Corps. But we were going to build a simple shed for ranch machinery, and I agreed to hire this boy to help us.

Now, we barely needed one boy, so I was a little shaken when three showed up. They were driving a rattletrap car from someplace back East. They'd been hitting the rock festivals and their hair was down on their shoulders.

Here, in masculinity-proving land, long hair is considered not only threat but anathema. Young cowboys take pleasure shaving "hippies" if they catch them in town on Saturday night. Narrow and provincial it is, but in Rome, the Romans; I tried to explain local prejudice to the eastern boys. I was the soul of diplomatic appeasement, pointing out gingerly that neither Harry Lovatt, the carpenter, nor my foreman and I liked long hair in this environment. Because I was making a job for these kids, at the substandard wage of one dollar per hour, I felt it was within my purlieu to ask them to trim up, be "clean for Gene" to work here.

It was a dastardly blow which they took under advisement. Moodily they finally got scissors and did some snipping, going from a shoulder-length haircut, say, to a pageboy. I was furious, and Pete, of course, was crestfallen by his tyrant father revealed. It was the Fourth of July weekend, so he escaped with the boys, plus four of our horses, bacon, wine, on a camp-out in the timber. They caught fish, emptied the wine and pondered on the savage world they'd come into.

On Tuesday morning, report-to-work time, the kids trooped back to my office. They announced that their hair was more important than the job. They were returning East, a quick round trip.

"Fine with me," I said, "if that's how you want it. Do you have travel money?"

Oh yes, they had bread. Then they made the mistake of sitting down at breakfast with Teddy. I was almost embarrassed at the way she lectured them. They kept saying, "But we're only kids. We don't have to accept responsibility yet."

"What do you mean you're only kids?" she cried. "You could be having a family, making a living, dying for your country."

They tiptoed away, visibly shaken. Down the road about seventy miles, they stopped for gas. The kid with the longest hair got out of the car and said, "I'm going back."

He walked at least twenty miles, because nobody would pick him up with the hairdo; they don't, out here. Finally a truck gave him a lift and he arrived at the ranch about dark, his feet blistered. He cut his hair and went to work, helped build the shop. When it was done, Harry said to me, "That kid is the best worker I've had in a long time. I'd hire him any day."

I don't know if we helped that boy, or set him back in his search for himself. But I do believe in a few weeks he grew toward manhood, simply because somebody had challenged him.

A few weeks later another older boy and girl dropped by. They'd finished college and were angrily idealistic. They'd just come from the People's Park ruckus at Berkeley. They were dedicated to the youth revolution and were working at it in grim ghetto jobs.

I admired their ardor. But we hadn't talked long before I appeared to them as somebody whose thought process was rooted down in his jackboots. The dialogue got pretty snappish: one of those weary political arguments where you throw your facts, I throw mine; finally it doesn't matter, it's my ego versus yours. I went to bed and resolved there'd be no more politics if we wanted to stay under the same roof.

Then a strange thing happened. Our talk drifted to books and ranch life; we rode cattle together and went fishing. At the end of three days the bearded young fellow glanced at me while we were unsaddling the horses. "You know, Mr. Carney," he said, "we've truly enjoyed this time here, seeing how you live. I envy you. Because what you want is exactly what we want. But you've done it. You've broken with the system. You've done your thing."

As they drove away, I was sorry to see them go. They'd taught me something, these kids; indeed, so many of them have who stop here at the ranch summer after summer just to visit. I could see in them what I'd wanted, too, as a youth. They were seeking identity as individuals; they yearned for the stimulation and challenge of making their own lives. They no longer saw this opportunity in a depersonalizing system of values that were often false, whether it be education, business or social life. They'd seen their parents, or me, come a cropper playing the game.

Indeed, some of these kids were bigoted and intense in their revolution, many of them so impassioned that they would throw away the freedoms we still had for the tragic and even more depersonalizing smother of an anarchy first, and finally a dreary Orwellian state. They didn't see it through to the end, those who wanted to smash the dream, burn it down, baby, and start again.

But they were that desperate to get out. I had been too. Our disagreement now was not in concept, only in method. As our own boys trooped up the ladder and into the welter of the college revolutions, I rued the emotional blood bath they were going through. But I didn't blame them for it. This was their time; they had to live it. And the Goliath system was rattling in their thunder, the cornices cracking. I could understand why they were angry; and Teddy and I had been as guilty for causing it as many other parents. We had trained, driven and tested these kids to push them into the "best colleges." Why? Because society said you must. Get the finest education. And what they found, when they came to it, was mostly an irrelevant farce.

Almost all the boys who came to the ranch felt they'd been cheated by college, saw it as a hypocritical treadmill of diplomas that taught them everything but how to think, how to savor the wisdom of man; trained them for nothing and turned them loose as despondent, jobless liberal-arts majors alienated from society and apparently having no constructive place in it. Further, they were frustrated by a political system that no longer represented its people. It was politics by the pressure groups, the best public relations, rob Peter to pay Paul and who cares about one man's vote. Beyond this was a future in some monolithic corporation, computers doing the work, the men "making work" in ritualistic jobs that had neither humanity nor freedom, only the satisfaction of bringing home a dollar to buy things with. And that buck reward was a house in the suburbs, connected by a ghastly commuting train, a rotting city you fled; and out in the peace of the sand traps, slash and keep slashing just to pay the bills.

I couldn't blame the kids for not wanting that world.

But there was hope in them. Despite the failure of their education, at least their idealism had been fired. The ones who survived, who didn't cop out on drugs or turn into bomb throwers for some police state, were indeed going to make the world a better place. They would not, as we'd done, troop sheeplike into the stamping mill. They wanted a new quality in their life; they wanted to *be,* in a spiritual sense; to be judged on being not doing, earning; dedicating themselves to man and the freedom of their existence as individuals. If they had the courage to persevere, the guts to build enough self-discipline (this would be the test!), then they would become their own Thoreaus. And become instruments for a spiritual revolution where each man, unique as his own creation, could live the dream of his soul.

Futuristic, utopian? Yes. But something *is* happening. There's a rumbling beneath us; we feel it even here. New people are coming in, not many, but perhaps a start. Here's a young graduate of a good eastern college: he's now a blacksmith and he runs the ski tow in the winter. No money in that life, but enough to get by and find a true, unique sense of satisfaction. Or another

163

man, a fine musician and a painter: he'd recorded for many of the big bands. Now he prowls the woods and paints landscapes, teaches music and art to pay for his simple needs. While sitting in his apartment in New York, he'd picked out this wilderness by jabbing his finger on a road map. Then he wrote the Chamber of Commerce and the letter ended up with me. I told him how to get here.

Others, too, are coming. One old friend shot an antelope on the ranch and we fished together. Now he owns a bigger ranch a few miles from us, spends months here.

And in tomorrow's mail there'll be a letter, or next week the phone will ring. Some old friend from some city, reaching that age where you search for new values. The kids are gone, now it's just us, you tell your wife. Shall we begin to live?

The end here is always in the
fall. The kids have returned to
their colleges; the tourists have
dragged dusty campers down the highways to the cities. September flashes wild,
violent in the equinoctial storm; it rains,
snows, then melts off, but still the battlements of
the Wind Rivers begin to look icy-bleak, humping
down for the onslaught soon to come.

Wyoming will be ours now, Teddy and me. People
ask: What do you do with yourselves—just sit in this little
room, two red leather chairs by the rock fireplace, and stare
at each other?

Yes, that's about it. We happen to love that stare; the warmth
of it as you glance up from a book. Or walk in the Indian summer
moon down to the bridge. Come back inside, light a pipe. No, the
phone won't be ringing, and the so-and-so's won't be stopping off
on their way to Yellowstone. Nobody comes. Just us. But maybe
we've waited a long time for this, twenty-three years. The rest of
the people have been pleasant diversions, beloved kids, but all
just passing through.

This afternoon Teddy and I have been out riding in the sagebrush. The splendor of it won't leave me now, so I pick up water-
colors and try to capture it, stare from the crackling of the fire to
my pathetically childish sketch. I'm still at the second-grade
level of art. But it's mine, this smear of color, lumpy people and
papier-mâché mountains. And for the hours I spend in my crude
sloppings, time is turned off; I'm totally committed to a dream.
Nobody'll ever judge it, let alone buy it. That's the good part. It's
just for me.

But the real unfolding of our life is its mixture of the men-
tal and the physical. It's creativity and contemplation insu-
lated from the world; the next moment, action, struggle, outside.
Work, exhaustion, frustration, anger, very much in the world.
That's what I try to explain to the people who come here in the
fall.

This now is a yearly occurrence for us: we invite some of our
old friends from the East or California. Afternoons before they
arrive, I slog out through the duck marshes, getting an idea
where the birds are working this year. I peer into the pools on the

river, hoping that a particularly fine brook trout will be lying in exactly this spot the morning we float.

But when our friends arrive, they don't seem to care if that trout moved or the geese didn't dump down just where I reconnoitered. They've come to share our life for these few days, find out what it really means. Are we happy here? Could they be? In trying to answer some of their questions, I evolved this book. The idea had been circling me for a long time, but I wasn't ready yet. I wasn't really sure.

"Come along with us," I tell them. "Tomorrow pretty well sums it up."

The alarm goes off at five-thirty. I hate, for any reason, getting up before a civilized hour. But Teddy goads me out of bed and slips on her long underwear. She's younger-looking and trimmer than she was fifteen years ago, never seems tired now. The frailty of woman is a myth; as the Indians well knew, squaws can outwork a man every time, if you're wise enough to give them the chance. Then we gulp down a breakfast and I look outside. There's ice fringing the river on the fifth of October. Beyond, the lights are on in Dave's house and out at the barns. Like dark lumps on the hay meadows, I can see hundreds of yearlings. They don't know it yet, but this is the day of reckoning for all of us. Soon fifteen big diesel trucks will rumble in; we'll weigh the yearlings and know whether we've won or lost.

When we go out in the dark to the corral, our horses stare at us with cold hatred. We've been working these cow ponies hard for days now, and their union rules tell them they've about had enough. Teddy's palomino chooses this morning not to come to grain. "You sonofabitch," I breathe, "get in that corral." He whirls, snorts. Finally I slide my arm around his neck, get a bridle on and saddle up. Then I catch my horse. He's an easy catch, but he's got a temper streak in him, stands humped up. When I get on, he spins a little, his body tense under me. It can't be more than fifteen degrees; he's snorting frost. As we trot toward the bridge, a moose comes out of the willows. My horse shies and trembles. It would simplify his day if he could pitch me off right now.

He knows what's ahead. We join Dave and Mike and young Davy too, kept home from school. Everybody stays home from school here at cattle-shipping time: first things first. We ride out into the meadows, the sun beginning to crack over the mountains, mist rising. A pair of sandhill cranes warble off ahead of us; then those wily geese . . . a whole flock of them honk and splash up from the slough. (I never figured them to be hiding there! Now I've lost them for my hunters.)

Trotting, we split up, Teddy going into the willows on the far side of the meadows. We're all beginning to whoop and holler at the cattle. They come slogging out, peering at us. God, they look thin! And there goes one, oh hell . . . limping; we've doctored his foot rot all summer and it's still not cured. The buyer will turn him back, deduct two hundred and some dollars from that check we're counting on.

Soon the yearlings are stringing out ahead of us. We move gingerly. Dave hollers at Davy or Teddy, "Don't crowd 'em!" Yeah, please don't. We work all year, suffer these beasts through sickness and death; if they break now, start a stampede, you could run off hundreds of pounds. But there are always two or three who start drifting away from the herd. You have to anticipate them, keep your horse not too close, not too far, just a shadow in their eye. You stupid bastards, I breathe, you've seen that gate fifty times. Now go through it.

The rebels break, gamboling off up through the hay meadows, kicking, ringing their tails. My horse bites out toward them, ears pinned back, trying to head them. We fly, leaping an irrigation ditch, the wind drying my eyes and parching my throat, the yearlings now racing flat out—stubborn devils, won't stop. Then, caught, they plant their sharp hooves, whirl; my horse cuts to them, my vertebrae lurch and lock, but the cattle are turned. The others are milling through the gate, and these, their sport over, trot back to join them. Poor man's fox hunt.

Then we crowd them into the log alleys that Dave and the kids have built; the yearlings are humping up on each other's backs, bawling, hundreds of them jammed in the narrow weighing chute. Out of the corner of my eye I see our friends from the cities: they're up now, walking toward the corrals with their cameras.

But at the same instant, one steer, crowded too close, cuts back up the corral. He wants to get out into the meadows again. His eyes are red, he's in panic. We try to turn him, but he makes a horrendous leap against the woven-wire fence, bounces off with a sickening thud and lies still. Dave wheels off his horse, kicks the steer in the butt. The animal gets up, stiff-legged, dazed. He's bleeding at the nose. We listen, and now we can hear him breathe. It's a whistling sound. Broken nose. They'll hear that too, the buyers. Turn him back, another two hundred and ten bucks.

By now the first diesel trucks are beginning to pull in to the chute. The buyers have also arrived, three corn farmers in a tan Lincoln with Iowa plates. They greet us, grinning, frosty breaths: "How much they going to weigh?"

"Awful light," I say. Hoping, fat as hell.

The buyers now have the option: shall we weigh these and load them off for the railroad; or do they want to wait until we gather the next five hundred out of the upper meadows? (If these first yearlings mill around a pen, no food or water, for another forty minutes, they'll lose a lot of pounds. The buyers ought to like this.) But they're decent fellows. "We'll weigh these and get them off," they call to me. "Then we can warm up while you're gathering the others."

We dismount stiffly and go into the scale house. My hands are numb; I dig out a stub of a pencil and paper, but each of the buyers has his own official-looking tally sheets. The first ten steers are shoved and cussed onto the scale, the gate slammed. Dave operates the scale slide, shoots it up to 7500 lbs., clunk, down she goes, too much. Slide it back, 73,72,70 . . . 69, ouch. It quivers there. "That good for you fellers?" Dave asks.

"About 690 pounds"—one buyer grins—"those are the right kind."

I glance at Dave. Goddammit, we both think, they should be running about 730. What the hell has happened? Dave mutters, "There was a couple of runty little buggers in that load. We'll get into some better ones pretty quick."

"I sure hope so."

Ten yearlings at a time, and we're going to have to do it a hundred times before the day is done. Punch the weigh tickets, give the buyers a copy, keep one ourselves. The weights do inch up; I almost want to reach out and hug some of those broad-backed chunky steers. Then one of the buyers, who's been out in the corral, nudges me. "Say," he says, "there are four or five out here that have horns."

"Yes, there are." We look at each other. There's a cloud over the sun now; maybe it'll snow.

"I can't use 'em with horns," he says. "Not at this price."

I know what he's thinking: cattle with horns will bruise the flesh of others when they're jammed in the trucks. But it's really just a buyer's ploy, knock off a few dollars. My face feels hot; I flare. "They had horns on 'em last summer when you saw them, when you contracted."

He lights a cigarette and goes back to talk to the other buyers. They watch the weights of a few more loads. Then the head buyer comes back to the scale house. "Well, we'll take those few with the horns. They won't hurt. But there is one out there with a broken nose. And another with foot rot."

"I know. Cut 'em back."

An hour later they're loaded and gone. We're riding out in the hay meadows for the next five hundred, heifers this time. And young Davy Shannon trots his horse up between his father and me. He's grinning. "Them guys," he says, "figured they was so smart, catching that foot rot and the broken nose. They never even seen them two that look like they're getting big brisket, and that one dinky broccle-faced thing we shoulda hit on the head."

Dave and I don't answer. "Well, Otis," Davy says, "how'd they do?"

"Not so good, Davy. Right at seven. Should have had thirty more pounds on 'em."

"That one storm a couple of days ago," Dave adds, "cost us a few thousand dollars, cold as the nights were."

Then Mike Shannon and Teddy ride up. They think the heifers will do better. But I'm sunk now. The sun is gone, snow showers bluish over the sage hills to the west. "It's hard," a friend told me once, "to beat a dollar out of a cow."

Damn hard. As I look back toward the ranch road, the diesels are throbbing away, taking the yearlings back to an Iowa cornfield: those people will make money with them. Moodily I slog ahead through the willows into the far meadows. You can't be very smart to spend your life and dreams on two of the oldest, most underpaid professions in the world: the pasturing of beasts and the telling of tales.

And yet, as we jog ahead toward the heifers, I pull my horse off toward a big slough. Mallards in it now, gorging on the weeds.

And I remember—when was it: not this summer, the one before
. . . before? Anyway, riding out there in the dusk with Tom, John
and Pete. A black bull had gotten in our heifers. We were trying
to run him out, the kids on their horses, racing, leaping sloughs,
hollering at each other, finally pranging him through a four-
wire fence and running him off. Not important. Just something
we did together and chuckled at as we rode home in the dusk.

The lowest-paid professions? Yes, but what was pay compared to those times? Or to Teddy, across the meadow from me
now, and Mike with her, whistling, whooping at the heifers. How
many men had their wives and family beside them, as I'd had?
A common struggle, never quite winning; but doing was all that
mattered. Chasing a dream, and realizing *that,* right there, was
the whole ball game.

I couldn't predict the cattle market; far wiser men had tried.
Less could I predict the entertainment audience. Why, for instance, should Sam Eagle, a symbol of the frontier I loved,
emerge to me in Utah from a cave, then transform to Mexico in
1916, and finally come out in a manuscript four publishers turned
down? Time passes, the game goes on. Then a call comes from
Hollywood: a producer has optioned Sam Eagle as a movie; another publisher says yes, they think there is appeal in him for a
book. Now.

What's now or what's yesterday? What man can predict all
these fates? Not I, surely. I begin to look in a mirror, and the boys,
my cowhands, are not riding this slough with me any more. But
I see them in me, life proceeding backward. Tom—God bless my
old pal and boss, Jack Webb—Jack hired Tom in Hollywood on
*Dragnet,* and taught him the film business for a summer. And an
architect friend from Princeton took John under his wing and
gave him a summer of designing houses; he told me, "If that boy
wants a full-time job, he's got it with us." And finally Pete, accepted at the small and desirable Colorado College. In fact, they
accepted him so early that Pete forgot to send in his acceptance
form. It arrived two days too late. Colorado College said sorry,
you've lost your place. We'll take you next fall.

"Oh God," Teddy groaned, "after all the anguish of getting
that boy through school and into a fine college . . ."

But maybe Pete's smarter than all of us. He's turned into a
superb photographer, and now for a year he's a working man, got

himself a job on the daily Rock Springs *Rocket Miner:* photographer and reporter, eighty bucks a week. College can wait for an experience like that. And Tom was with Pete for the summer, also a reporter; he's writing short stories now, working on them at night after he leaves the paper at ten-thirty P.M. I knew another dreamer who did the same. And John, not home: he's in California, doing the sound track on a movie at Stanford.

So what is now, or what's yesterday? It's just this moment, really, trotting the heifers back to the corral, knowing none of it matters, not when you can feel the new snow on your face, a tired honest horse beneath you: when you're no longer afraid to be, and feel.

"Why, those doggone heifers"—Dave beams when we total it up—"they went six hundred and fifty-seven pounds, average. I didn't figure them for six and a quarter, did you?"

"I sure didn't. Thanks, Dave . . . all of you. We'll make it, I think. Won't break the bank, but we'll come out."

By now our friends have shot their roll of film; some of them are already back at the house warming up. I never carry a watch, so I ask Teddy the time. "My God," she says, "do you realize it's two o'clock?"

Inside the house, the cow buyers have already been poured bourbon; they're gathered around the fire with our friends. Even with my long underwear on I'm frozen, warm up with a glass of whiskey that explodes right to my brain. Teddy has a lunch brewing, but the buyers and I aren't hungry yet; that is, we're ravenous, but we've got to settle up first. Everybody wants to know the totals. The brand inspector, an old-time cowboy, hulks into my office with us; we go over the brands, the final count of steers and heifers. Then we begin totting up the weigh slips on my adding machine. At first there's a mistake or two; the buyers have their pads out; we trade around and finally we agree. I grin and hand them complimentary Cowputers, but my fingers are too tense to operate my own damn invention. The Cowputer is great for estimates, but now we've got to have hard dollars and cents. There's no sound in my office except an occasional man picking up his whiskey glass. We multiply, all separately. The head buyer grins. "Well, my total," he says, "is one hundred and eighty-two thousand, six hundred sixty-one dollars and eighteen cents."

Another buyer says his comes to fourteen cents.

"Keep the change," somebody cracks.

My multiplication is close, slower than theirs; but I'm not looking at it. I know, burned into my mind, the total amount of money borrowed on the cattle, plus the interest, plus how much I need to pay the mortgage and operate for another year. I blow a long breath. Barely. We have barely covered everything, maybe around a thousand dollars' real profit. Then my heart soars— wait a minute: we can sell the few cutbacks for another thousand. But I look out the window, the damn ranch road: we're going to have to put a good three or four thousand into it to make it passable. And winter coming? Suppose the county no longer plows us out? They've threatened to quit all these private roads. Can we afford a small Cat . . . second-hand Cat . . . ? Of course we can't.

"Darling," Teddy cries, "when do you want to have lunch? You're going hunting this afternoon, aren't you?"

Are we ever!

The buyer, with a little checkbook like a woman uses at a supermarket, scribbles out the X thousand dollars. Something unreal about it, his bank paying my bank, and the little left over already more than spent. Trying to be casual, I drop the check into my file box with the unpaid bills and unborn story ideas. We shake hands. I hope you'll come back next year, I grin, after these cattle make a fortune for you.

Then a quick lunch for all of us; the buyers leave and my old friends bundle into the truck with their guns and rods. I split them up. Some of the men go into the black timber for grouse; I take a couple of the girls to the beaver ponds. They really don't know how to fly fish, but they try gamely. These are big trout. They're too smart for amateurs. "All right," I say to these beloved gals, "you've got a spinning rod there. These fish have never seen a junk lure. They're deep, too deep for flies. Bomb that hardware in there."

One of the girls smiles. "Now come on, we don't want to do it *that* way!"

"That's what they're here for. Catch one for me, will you?"

She arches out the first cast. There's a flash of silver in the black pond, a crimson-sided rainbow leaping, splashing, running line. I'm as excited as if I have him on myself. "Play him slow, don't let him get in the weeds."

She brings him in deftly, and the other old friend gets another on the next cast . . . superb, firm-fleshed trout about two and a half pounds.

That's enough for them. They're flushed with joy. One of them, as we walk back down the stream, says, "My God, Ote, how did you ever find such a place!"

A shotgun booms in the distance; my dogs come thumping toward us, followed by the hunters leaving the timber. Just one grouse, but they saw a couple of elk and five deer. We're not shooting big game. But we have no mercy on the ducks. In a snow shower, we go to the marsh where Teddy and I planted feed. We surround it, crawl through the sagebrush. The birds erupt: widgeon, mallard, redheads, bluebills and three honking geese. The guns spit fire in the dusk; the birds circle; we miss some, a few fall, our Labs splashing into the marsh. And now, startled from some slough, the three swans that live here fly overhead against the leaden orange-streaked sky. No one speaks. We stare at them and hear the beat of their wings, fading away.

In the evening, we're exhausted. We linger over dinner and wine, the fire crackling, then brandy to keep us awake. We go upstairs to shoot a game of pool: three-ball cowboy, the game of the ranch. I feel like an arm-weary fighter. I'm totally limp and at peace.

When we come back to the wives downstairs, they're talking about their world, with Teddy. The men mingle in for a time, too. It never gets very serious, doesn't have to with old friends like these. We remember people in common: did we hear that so-and-so's a hopeless drunk; and that the XYZ's have gotten their divorce, both remarried? Or that Joe or Bill or Charlie made it big to head up the company? Sorry, hadn't heard that either. Kind of out of touch. By now we're all yawning, and reluctantly we start for bed.

It's over then. The morning comes too soon. Gone are their hunting caps and boots; cameras put away. There's a fresh snow on the ground, and these old friends have thousands of miles to travel. Will the planes fly? What about the roads? Unfortunately, they've got to get back to a schedule. The doctor has a patient going into surgery next morning; the businessmen have meetings. They sign their names in our guest book, and then, after we've slid their coolers with birds and fish into the trunk of the Hertz car, we shake hands and embrace. "Aren't you ever going to come back our way?" they ask. "You've got to have some reason to come East. Or West."

"Oh, sure," I say. "We'll be coming."

One old friend smiles at me. "I don't know why you would . . . and leave this."

They get into their rented car and we wave goodbye again. I hate parting from ones you love. But at least it's over, I think. They rattle across our cattle guard. Then the car begins to buck and belch exhaust. It stops, the motor dead. I run out to them and begin my standard lecture: we can send men to the moon, but no auto manufacturer has figured out how to make a carburetor operate at 7600 feet. "Press the accelerator all the way to the floor," I say. "Burn hell out of it."

They try but don't quite have the pesky knack. So I get in and race the engine for them, finally driving them to the bridge: by now the carburetor mixture has by-passed the choke and is burning properly. I holler goodbye and they rock across the bridge, waving out the back window.

I stand on the bridge and watch them hurry away. They're the last. From now on, it's the big open, the quiet. The football games they go to aren't broadcast here; their *Wall Street Journal* gets to me three days late, if then. Come back, they say, come back to the trains and the companies and the chase.

In the first years, when they left, I'd feel a lump in my throat. Part of me did go back with them. And I'd yearn for that part I'd grown up in and later the excitement of California. It would tear at me in a gnawing loneliness, when I'd see the world I must make alone here.

But you can't have both.

The geese say this; they're beginning to honk restlessly on the bend of the river below. No hunting today. Or might I just sneak off? Or take the tractor and beat sagebrush? Put in wood for the winter? Soon, now, the river freezing, get out old hockey skates and rumble for miles on black ice, see the brook trout beneath, skittering away. And then, the vast whiteness, silence, no sound but the sluff of our skis. Dreams ahead: so much to do, so much to feel.

The trail doesn't go back across the bridge any more. It leads up the river to the rock fort and the blessed freedom, in this moment, thanks to God, finally ours.

## About the Author

For an intimate portrait of the author,
one should refer to this book.
Vital statistics at the simplest level
are that he was born in Chicago,
graduated from Princeton University,
served for two years as a captain
in the United States Marine Corps Reserve
in the South Pacific area, and has been
both a successful writer and rancher.
He lives now in Wyoming with his wife and,
occasionally, his three sons.